MW01091656

MODERN TAIWANESE AIR POWER, The Republic of Ch

Roy Choo and Peter Ho

MODERN TAIWANESE AIR POWER

The Republic of China Air Force Today

Roy Choo and **Peter Ho**

HARPIA
PUBLISHING+

Copyright © 2021 Harpia Publishing VerlagsGmbH
Meynertgasse 8/8, 1090 Wien, Austria
enquiries@harpia-publishing.com

All rights reserved.

No part of this publication may be copied, reproduced, stored electronically or transmitted in any manner or in any form whatsoever without the written permission of the publisher.

Consulting and inspiration by Kerstin Berger

Front cover artwork by Ugo Crisponi, Aviation Graphic shows an F-CK-1D armed with the Wan Chien cruise missile.

Rear cover artworks by Ugo Crisponi, Aviation Graphic show, from top to bottom: Mirage 2000-5EI, P-3C Orion and C-130HE Hercules.

Editorial by Thomas Newdick

Layout by Norbert Novak

Maps by James Lawrence

Printed at finidr, Czech Republic

Harpia Publishing is a member of

ISBN 978-1-950394-03-6

REPUBLIC OF CHINA AIR FORCE

Contents

Introduction: a force in transition

Between July 1995 and March 1996, the world watched as a crisis brewed across the Taiwan Strait. The 1995–96 Taiwan Strait crisis, as the events, came to be known, was sparked by a visit to the United States in June 1995 by the late Taiwan (officially the Republic of China, ROC) President Lee Teng-hui. China reacted furiously to the visit and flexed its military muscles. The People's Liberation Army (PLA) conducted a series of military exercises near Taiwan, simulating an invasion. It fired volleys of short-range ballistic missiles (SRBMs) close to the ports of Keelung and Kaohsiung, disrupting air and shipping links.

The fear that the exercises could develop into actual military action sparked panic among the Taiwanese. Taiwan's Republic of China Armed Forces was put on high alert. In the lead-up to Taiwan's first Presidential election in March 1996, which China was trying to influence with its 'missile blockade', the United States intervened by directing two carrier battle groups to the area. Further aggression was averted as parties expressed a willingness for reconciliation.

The eight-month crisis was the closest China and Taiwan had come to full-blown conflict since the Strait Crises of the 1950s. Beijing's military manoeuvres demonstrated how the introduction of SRBMs has changed the nature of a possible war over the Taiwan Strait. Taiwanese defence planners realised a missile attack, which it had no credible defence against, could devastate most of its military assets without physically engaging in actual fighting. This apprehension set about the development of Taiwan's revolution in military affairs, emphasising command, control, communications, computers, intelligence, surveillance and reconnaissance (C4ISR), missile defence as well as offensive capabilities.

For China, the inability to counter the US Navy carriers and having to halt its intimidation of Taiwan caused embarrassment. It accelerated the development of anti-access/area denial (A2/AD) capabilities and provided further impetus to the modernisation of its air power, which had been sparked by lessons learnt from the air campaign of the 1991 Gulf War. Beijing's leaders at that time also learnt that military coercion was counterproductive and set a strategy of wining the hearts and minds of Taiwanese through closer economic and cultural ties, while still harshly opposed to any calls of independence from the mainland.

Twenty-five years on, memories of the crisis might have faded but its implications live on today. China has emerged as a global power, its meteoric economic growth powering the strength of its military. Chinese President and General Secretary of the Chinese Communist Party (CCP) Xi Jinping has made reunification with Taiwan a centrepiece of his vision to restore China's wealth and power, possibly by 2049 – the year the People's Republic of China (PRC) turns 100. Under Xi, an increasingly assertive China has an expanding toolbox of economic, diplomatic and military measures, the latter of which he has been increasingly willing to threaten against Taiwan.

The PLA modernisation, of which air power has been a major beneficiary, has grave ramifications for Taiwan's widening military gap with China. Its first line of defence – the ROC Air Force (ROCAF) – not only has to content with the threat of a missile attack on the ability of its aircraft to respond, but also the steady decline in the balance of air superiority over the Taiwan Strait.

While the ROCAF did have the edge in air superiority at the turn of the century with the induction of Lockheed Martin F-16A/Bs, Dassault Mirage 2000-5s and indigenous

AIDC F-CK-1A/Bs, this proved to be temporary. The deployment by the PLA of local derivatives of the Russian Sukhoi Su-27 and Su-30 – the Shenyang J-11, J-15 and J-16 – as well as indigenously developed J-10 and J-20 have eroded this advantage and swung it in their favour. While the majority of the ROCAF's fighter fleet have been put through or are currently undergoing a mid-life upgrade, Taiwan's decade-plus-long attempts to acquire a new fighter were met with failure, further widening the fighter gap. The 2019 purchase of 66 F-16C/D Block 70 fighters for delivery between 2023 and 2026 will bring about the capability boost it desperately needs.

Cross-strait tensions have re-erupted following independence-leaning Tsai Ing-wen's election as Taiwan's President in 2016. In response, China has been conducting what it calls 'island encirclement' drills randomly since then, flying Xian H-6 bombers, escort fighters and support aircraft around Taiwan.

While Beijing's sabre-rattling has been the 'new normal' in recent years, 2020 saw a surge in PLA air activity in the vicinity of Taiwan, putting significant pressure on the ROCAF's airmen and machines. According to the Ministry of National Defense, more than 380 sorties alone were flown into the southwestern corner of Taiwan's Air Defence Identification Zone (ADIZ) over the course of the year. Most notably, tensions reached a worrying level over a weekend in mid-September when more than two dozen PLA fighters crossed the median line of the Taiwan Strait in response to an official United States visit. Analysts said tensions have never been higher since the 1995-96 Taiwan Strait crisis.

At this stage, while Beijing might not want a conflict due to the prohibitive costs to its economy and international reputation, should things continue on current trajectory, the risk of one in the next decade will be high. However, as China steps up the employment of grey-zone tactics while Taiwan ramps up air patrols in return, inadvertent escalations could occur, and rationality sometimes does not prevail in such situations.

In the face of the overwhelming air threat and the array of weaponry the PLA has at its disposal, the ROCAF will have to find ways to remain credible in the defence of Taiwan's airspace. Taiwan's Ministry of Defence (MND) is implementing the Overall Defense Concept (ODC), an asymmetric defence strategy, that could better position Taiwan's military to not only survive in an all-out conflict but also slow and attrite the invading force. As we shall see in the book, new capabilities the ROCAF will induct could form the basis of this asymmetric strategy.

This book is divided into five parts: the origins and early years of the ROCAF; a review of the ROCAF's force structure; an analysis of its air power strategy; a study of the current aircraft fleet; and Taiwan's future air power prospects.

Roy Choo and Peter Ho, April 2021

Acknowledgements

The authors would like to thank the many individuals who have assisted in the publication of this work in one way or other, be it the frank discussions on Taiwanese air power, the contribution of images and artwork and the reviewing of the book. Heartfelt thanks should also go to their family and loved ones for their understanding and patience throughout the research and writing process, during what was a very challenging period, including Stephan de Bruijn, Huang Yang-te 'Mango', Collin Koh, Gert Kromhout, Eric Lai, Kitsch Liao, Wendell Minnick and Todd Shugart.

中　華　民　國　空　軍

Abbreviations

A2/AD	anti-access/area denial
ADIZ	Air Defence Identification Zone
AEW	airborne early warning
AIDC	Aerospace Industrial Development Corporation
ARG	Air Rescue Group
ATRDC	Aerospace Technology Research and Development Centre
C²	comand and control
C4ISR	command, control, communications, computers, intelligence, surveillance and reconnaissance
CAP	combat air patrol
CCK	Ching Chuan Kang Air Base
CCP	Chinese Communist Party
CW	Combined Wing
DCA	defensive counter-air
DOD	Department of Defense (USA)
EWG	Early Warfare Group
FMS	Foreign Military Sales
FTW	Flight Training Wing
GBAD	ground-based air defence
JSOW	Joint Stand-Off Weapon
LOROP	long-range oblique reconnaissance
MAAG	Military Advisory Assistance Group
MAP	Military Assistance Program
MND	Ministry of National Defence
NCSIST	National Chung-Shan Institute of Science and Technology
OCU	operational conversion unit
ODC	Overall Defence Concept
OTEG	Operational Test & Evaluation Group
PLA	People's Liberation Army
PLAAF	People's Liberation Army Air Force
PLARF	PLA Rocket Force
PRC	People's Republic of China
ROC	Republic of China (Taiwan)
ROCAF	Republic of China Air Force
RRR	rapid runway repair
SRMB	short-range ballistic missile
TAG	Tactical Airlift Group
TCW	Tactical Combined Wing
TFG	Tactical Fighter Group
TFW	Tactical Fighter Wing
THAAD	Terminal High Altitude Area Defense
TRG	Tactical Reconnaissance Group
USD	US Dollar

THE REPUBLIC OF CHINA AIR FORCE – ORIGINS AND EARLY YEARS

Roy Choo and *Peter Ho*

The Republic of China Air Force (ROCAF) is among the oldest air forces in the world, having marked its 100th anniversary on 29 November 2020. While the focus of this book is its current form and capabilities, we will not have a full appreciation of the organisation without understanding its rich legacy – something that is not widely accessible or understood in Western literature.

This chapter provides an introduction to the storied history of the ROCAF and some noteworthy details of its past.

Beginning of the ROCAF

The ROCAF, as we know it today, was formally established as the Aviation Ministry on 29 November 1920. With the Japanese invasion of Manchuria in 1931, the Chinese central government under Chiang Kai-shek began the organisation of its military. Air units from various warlords were integrated into the Chinese Nationalist Air Force. Beginning in 1937, the War of Resistance against the Japanese saw Chinese pilots fight valiantly while heavily outnumbered. A major victory occurred on 14 August 1937, when three Japanese Mitsubishi G3M bombers were shot down during a raid on Hangzhou with no losses. As the episode occurred in such a desperate time, 14 August was proclaimed as Air Force Day and is still celebrated to this day.

1949–1969

Following the end of the War of Resistance, the Chinese Civil War broke out in 1946 between the Nationalists and the Communists. The air force was hardly used in the conflict till 1950 after the ROC government established itself in Taiwan. While the ROCAF had piston-driven aircraft, the People's Liberation Army Air Force (PLAAF) had jet fighters in the form of Mikoyan Gurevich MiG-15s. The establishment of the United States Military Advisory Assistance Group (MAAG) helped to address this disadvantage as military aid, including superior aircraft and training, were delivered. The ROCAF's first jet fighters, the Republic F-84G Thunderjets, were delivered in June 1953. This was followed by North American F-86F Sabres which arrived in December 1954.

A pair of F-86F Sabres in Thunder Tiger markings and armed with AIM-9B Sidewinder missiles, at Tainan Air Base some time in the 1960s. The introduction of the F-86 provided the ROCAF with a much superior fighter over its mainland adversaries and helped achieve a high kill ratio during the 1958 Strait Crisis. (MND)

The 1958 Taiwan Strait Crisis saw encounters between PLAAF MiG-15s and ROCAF F-86Fs. The first employment of air-to-air missiles was made in September that year when AIM-9 Sidewinders were used by the F-86s. The ROCAF's first supersonic fighter, the North American F-100 Super Sabre was also delivered in October 1958.

In 1960, the ROCAF received the first of many Lockheed F-104 Starfighters under Project Alishan. Throughout the 1960s, the F-104s proved their worth by keeping the PLAAF at bay while RF-104Gs conducted reconnaissance flights around the coastal regions of the the mainland without any serious challengers.

In the late 1960s, the ROCAF also attained 118 Northrop F-5A/B Freedom Fighters delivered through the US Military Assistance Program. About half of these were diverted to Phillippines and South Vietnam air forces on the request of the United States.

The ROCAF 34th Squadron 'Black Bat' operated a variety of aircraft for its clandestine missions, including the Fairchild C-123K Provider supplied by the CIA. These were flown over Vietnam in support of the United States' war effort. (ROCAF GHQ)

Black units

At the behest of the United States Central Intelligence Agency (CIA), the ROCAF established two covert squadrons to conduct clandestine missions deep into Chinese territory during the Cold War. While the operations were fraught with danger and losses were heavy, they were seen as necessary to secure aid and support from the US.

Black Bat Squadron

The Special Operations Squadron (China Taskforce) was established in June 1952 at Taoyuan Air Base to conduct airborne missions 'behind enemy lines'. These included support of guerrilla operations, psychological warfare activities such as leaflet and food parcel airdrops and electronic intelligence (ELINT) missions. The unit relocated to Hsinchu Air Base in 1953 and was numbered the 34th Squadron in 1958, taking on the 'Black Bat' identity. The squadron emblem depicts a bat flying over the Big Dipper.

The squadron operated a large variety of aircraft including Douglas A-26, Boeing B-17, Lockheed P2V-7/RB-69, Douglas C-54, Fairchild C-123, Lockheed C-130, and Lockheed P-3A that had been converted for ELINT and air sampling.

A remarkable mission was conducted in May 1969 to spy on the PRC's nuclear weapons test program in Lop Nur. The CIA was keen to gather intelligence on the tests and developed a plan to deploy sensor pallets from a C-130E flown by a 'Black Bat' squadron crew. From Takhli Air Base in Thailand, the crew flew nap-of-the-earth and in the

Over 247 F-104s were received in 11 batches from various sources under Project Alishan, with many of these utilised for spares. Towards the end of its service, high accident and unavailability rates plagued the fleet. TF-104G 4184, a former West German example, crashed into the sea near the Matsu Islands on 11 August 1996. It was the last ROCAF F-104 to be lost. (Withheld via Peter Ho)

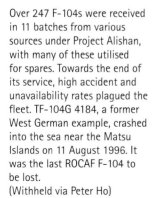

dark for six and a half hours. On reaching the target area at Mazong Mountain, the sensor pallets were dropped before making the return trip and arriving safely in Thailand.

The squadron shifted its focus to support the United States' Vietnam War effort in the later years, gathering intelligence on Viet Cong operations. When the unit was stood down in 1972, 838 missions had been flown while 148 crew members and 15 aircraft were lost, most of these attributed to enemy action.

Black Cat Squadron

Project Razor was formalised in 1958 on the back of the United States' increased appetite for intelligence on China's nuclear program. The program called for the establishment of a ROCAF U-2 squadron with Taiwan to contribute base facilities and pilots, while aircraft and crew training were to be furnished by the US.

The first batch of six ROCAF pilots – of an eventual 28 – arrived at Laughlin Air Force Base (AFB), Texas in March 1959 for training on the U-2. The first U-2C was delivered to Taoyuan Air Base in January 1961. The establishment of the 35th Squadron, nicknamed the Black Cat Squadron, took place in the following month, although the 'Air Force Meteorological Reconnaissance Research Group' was used as a cover.

The 'Black Cat' Squadron flew high-altitude strategic reconnaissance missions deep within Chinese territory to collect information on its nuclear and missile development programs. Losses to Chinese S-75 Dvina (ASCC SA-2 Guideline) surface-to-air missile (SAMs) and J-7 interceptors were so heavy that improved electronic countermeasures (ECM) equipment were installed despite initial reluctance from the US. As a result of the threat, the 'Black Cat' squadron no longer flew into the mainland after March 1968. Instead, it operated from a stand-off distance in international waters and employed its Long-Range Oblique Reconnaissance (LOROP) camera and electronic surveillance capabilities. The unit received the larger and more capable U-2R from April 1969.

The Sino-US rapprochement from 1974 brought about the cessation of 'Black Cat' activities in May that year. By the end of the ROCAF's U-2 operations, 220 reconnaissance missions had been flown. Six U-2s were lost during operations – five to enemy action and one due to a technical fault. Six further aircraft were lost during training sorties from Taoyuan. The 'Black Cats' paid a huge price for the high-risk missions they undertook – of the 28 trained pilots, four were killed in action, six were lost during training while a further two were captured and only released after nearly two decades. The 'Black Cat' identity lives on with the US Air Force's 5th Reconnaissance Squadron which operates the U-2 from Osan Air Base in South Korea.

The ROCAF U-2 crew paid a huge price for the high-risk missions they undertook. One third of the trained pilots were lost in reconnaissance missions and training.
(MND)

1970–1990

The licenced production of the F-5E/F Tiger II by Aero Industry Development Corporation, later Aerospace Industrial Development Corporation (AIDC) began under Project Hu An (Peace Tiger), with the first rolled out in 1974. Over the next 12 years, 308 F-5s would be produced in six batches from Peace Tiger 1 through 6.

The 1980s also saw Taiwan initiating work on the Indigenous Defence Fighter (IDF) project after the United States government refused to sell any fighter aircraft amid its newfound relationship with China. This project gave rise to the F-CK-1, which conducted its maiden flight in 1989.

Northrop T-38A Talons of the 8th Group overfly Hualien Air Base in the mid-1990s. The T-38 was flown by the ROCAF on two separate occasions. In 1972, 28 aircraft were loaned by the United States in exchange for the transfer of Taiwan's F-5As to South Vietnam. In 1995, 40 T-38s were once again leased to provide sufficient training aircraft in anticipation of the arrival of its second-generation fighters.
(Withheld via Peter Ho)

Assistance to Singapore's fledging air force

What is perhaps less well known – due to obscurity by both parties – is Taiwan's assistance to the Singapore's fledging air force between the early 1970s to the late 1980s.

When it was announced that the British military would withdraw from Singapore in 1971, the newly independent country faced an urgent task to build its armed forces. Assistance was sought from a handful of countries. Taiwan, keen to develop ties with Singapore, sent a proposal to help train its air force, which was taken up. The training program later became part of a more comprehensive Project Xing Guang (Starlight) military cooperation framework.

The first batch of four ROCAF flight instructors arrived in May 1973, initiating the assistance program to the Singapore Air Defence Command (later renamed the Republic of Singapore Air Force, RSAF). ROCAF pilots sent to Singapore were selected based on their flying proficiency and English fluency, typically serving for two and a half years in their instructor role. A number of technicians were also sent to assist with the set-up of aircraft maintenance units. The first four pilots were brought in to support Singapore's Douglas A-4S Skyhawk program; within months of their arrival, they were deployed to Naval Air Station Lemoore to receive platform-specific training from the US Navy (USN). Singapore's first two A-4S squadrons – 142 and 143 Squadrons – were set up in 1974 and 1975 respectively, with two of these pilots designated as commanding officers. Ironically, in what would have been the only foreign air force to have done so apart from the United States, a detachment of upgraded Singaporean A-4SU Super Skyhawks deployed to Chihhang Air Base, Taitung in 1992, flying alongside ROCAF F-5E/Fs.

With the rapid growth of Singapore's air force in the 1970s, more jet-trainers were required. One of the Taiwanese instructors led a team to France to acquire ex-French Air Force Lockheed T-33A Shooting Stars – a type the ROCAF also operated between 1957 and 1989. He subsequently set up the 131 Squadron with 20 of these aircraft. The initial cadre of instructors was also sent to Taiwan to receive training on ROCAF T-33s.

The assistance program entered a new phase from 1975 with Singapore's request for longer term instructor assignments. Taiwan acceded to this, provided deployed personnel would have already left the service of the ROCAF.

At least three former ROCAF officers were appointed to key staff positions in the RSAF. Among them was former ROCAF Major General Liu Ching-chuan, who served as the RSAF's Director Air Staff (subsequently renamed as the Chief of Air Force) from 1977 to 1980. The longest serving officer was Fu Chun-hsien, previously an F-86 and F-100 pilot, who spent over a decade in the RSAF and Singapore's defence ministry in a variety of senior staff positions.

The assistance program to Singapore concluded in the late 1980s, with over 50 Taiwanese officers and enlisted personnel having served in the RSAF. While many had the opportunity to remain in Singapore, all of them returned to Taiwan at the end of their service.

Fu Chun-hsien pictured after a sortie in an RSAF A-4S Skyhawk. (Fu Chun-hsien)

Great Desert program

Although the program has been declassified, Taiwan's assistance to the Yemen Arab Republic (colloquially North Yemen) between 1979 to 1990 is still shrouded in secrecy today. The Yemenite War of 1979 erupted between Yemen Arab Republic and the People's Democratic Republic of Yemen (South Yemen) after a period of strained relations. Saudi Arabia was keen to back its North Yemen ally against South Yemen, which had the support of the USSR and Egypt. It considered South Korea and Taiwan as countries that could provide training to support the build-up of North Yemen's air force.

The military aid program began with a request to Taiwan in March 1979. The United States had just severed relations with Taiwan and Saudi Arabia was its next largest diplomatic country, hence, this was a request that could not be refused. The program was known as Project Da Mo (Great Desert) to Taiwan and was financially supported by Saudi Arabia, which named it the Peace Bell Program. The United States delivered 12 Northrop F-5E Tiger IIs as military aid while Saudi Arabia supplied a further four twin-seat F-5Bs.

Taiwanese personnel deployed to the North Yemeni task group were issued Saudi Arabian passports and wore uniforms of the Saudi Arabian military. The first batch of 80 flight and ground crew arrived in Sana'a on 26 April 1979 and took on the task of operationalising the F-5 with 112 Squadron at Al-Dailami Air Base.

Taiwan's official stance of the program is that the ROCAF personnel were there only for the training of North Yemen's flight and maintenance crew. However, it is not inconceivable that during the early stages of the program, ROCAF pilots could have flown combat missions against the South Yemen Air Force which had Mikoyan-Gurevich MiG-21s and Sukhoi Su-22s in its fleet. Rumours persist of air-to-air kills scored in the weeks following the arrival of the task group.

The unification of Yemen and the termination of the Saudi Arabia-Taiwan relations in 1990 led to the end of the program. A total of about 700 ROCAF personnel were deployed to North Yemen over the 12-year span of the Project Great Desert, each member serving a one-year tour of duty. Many of them rose to senior military and civilian positions, including the late General Shen Yi-ming, who was Chief of the General Staff when he perished in a UH-60M crash on 2 January 2020.

AIDC F-CK-1 tail no. 1428
going transsonic. The Ching-kuo
was developed in line with the
country's policy of self-reliance
in defence technology after
it was not able to aquire the
fighter aircraft it required in
the late 1970s and early 1980s.
It was introduced into service
in 1992 as the ROCAF's first
second-generation fighter.
(Peter Ho)

1991–2000

The 1990s was a decade of opportunities and challenges for the ROCAF. A window of opportunity to purchase western third-generation aircraft opened in 1992, leading to the firming up of contracts for 150 F-16A/Bs and 60 Mirage 2000s. The first of 130 F-CK-1s were also delivered that year, heralding a new chapter for the ROCAF.

The air force would once again be tested during the 1995-96 Taiwan Strait crisis. With aging F-5E/Fs, an increasingly unreliable fleet of F-104s and less than one wing worth of F-CK-1s that had yet to attain full operational capability (FOC), it was recognised that the ROCAF was at its weakest and most threatened at this time. Tensions were high over the Taiwan Straits as the PLA conducted missile tests and probed the air defences of Taiwan, amidst large scale exercises simulating its invasion. Fortunately, the crisis was resolved peacefully.

The first of the F-16A/Bs and Mirage 2000s arrived in 1997. Together with the F-CK-1, these form – what it terms – its second-generation fighter fleet. Apart from enhanced capabilities such as beyond-visual-range (BVR) air-to-air missiles and precision guided munitions (PGM), pilots who had been detached overseas brought back not only knowledge on weapons and tactics but also different ideas and perspectives that would help take the organisation into the next century. With the new fighters, the last of the F-104s and large numbers of F-5s were withdrawn.

THE ROCAF TODAY

Roy Choo

The ROCAF, as the aviation branch of the ROC Armed Forces, is charged with wielding its air power capability to achieve operational, tactical and strategic objectives. It is the tip of the spear of the ROC military and is at the forefront of Taiwan's defence against a PLA air and missile threat or an invasion from across the straits.

Republic of China Air Force
(ROCAF) enblem

Mission and purpose

The security of Taiwan is inextricably linked to the control and exploitation of the air environment over and around the island. Taiwan's civilian and military leaders are keenly aware that if a conflict occurs and China is given free reign over Taiwan's airspace, the war would have been lost. The destruction of radars and missile defences mean that Taiwan will be more vulnerable to ballistic missile barrages. ROC Navy ships could not put out to sea safely to assert maritime control while troops, armoured fighting vehicles and helicopters of the ROC Army would be exposed to air attacks. Conversely, should the PLA air arms be unable to gain air dominance, any offensive effort will be held down by Taiwan's firepower and casualties of the invading force will be heavy.

According to the ROC National Defence Report 2019, a biannual Ministry of National Defence (MND) publication on its current security environment and national defence policy, the ROCAF's major strategic missions are to: 'conduct combat air patrols (CAPs) and maintain the security of the airspace over the Taiwan Strait; and 'seek to gain air dominance and join the ROC Army and Navy in various joint operations to exert their full potential'.

ROCAF's doctrines emphasise the conduct of air operations to secure air superiority. In the face of a superior aggressor, the doctrines stress the need to 'strive as much as possible for local air superiority in order to benefit the overall campaign'. The ability to control certain airspace at least temporarily will be crucial for the conduct of a whole host of other missions. As such CAP and defensive counter-air (DCA) would be the most crucial wartime missions for the ROCAF.

With the requirement to support the army and navy in their land and sea battles, the ROCAF will also be expected to perform transport and re-supply, air-to-ground and anti-ship/submarine missions. Increased emphasis by the defence establishment over

Republic of China roundel

Republic of China
low-visibility roundel

the past decade to grow a greater offensive and counter-force capability has also led the ROCAF fighter fleet to take on a stand-off strike mission set.

Operational structure

Currently the ROCAF has an approximate strength of 32,000 personnel, more than half its establishment in the 1990s of 65,000. The drastic reductions, which were part of an armed forces-wide downsizing and streamlining effort, were largely made in its support units while the strength of the operational units was mostly preserved.

With a much larger regular force, the ROCAF has also been less impacted compared to its sister services by MND's shift from mandatory conscripts to an all-volunteer force – the last of these year-long conscripts in the ROCAF were discharged in 2018. The ROCAF still accepts its share of conscripts from the four-month compulsory military training as well as reservists but their contribution is questionable with their short commitment period.

The ROCAF values the wealth of experience possessed by retired pilots and has put in place a scheme for veterans to return to the force as civilian instructor pilots. These personnel serve in instructor roles in various units, including in fighter squadrons. More recently, a 'weekend warrior program' was also established to allow retired personnel to report back to their previous units for duties up to several days per month.

The ROCAF headquarters is located in Dazhi district of Taipei city. Heading the organisation is an officer holding the rank of a three-star general. The administrative structure includes four major commands:

- **Combatant Command** – through the JAOC, responsible for the planning, command and control of the air defence of Taiwan by integrating the ROCAF combat and surveillance capabilities. Also oversee the provision of relevant flight operations support such as air traffic control and meteorological monitoring.
- **Education, Training and Doctrine Development Command** – responsible for the overall training and competencies of airmen as well as doctrine development. During combat operations, the command will function as a back-up Joint Air Operations Centre (JAOC) in the command and control of the defence of Taiwan's airspace.
- **Maintenance and Logistics Command** – oversees maintenance, supply and logistics functions to meet the operational requirements of the ROCAF
- **Air Defence and Artillery Command** – responsible for the ROCAF ground-based air defence (GBAD) forces. Taiwan's offensive missile capabilities are rumoured to be also assigned to this command.

Air bases and tenant organisations

As detailed in the order of battle as of April 2021, the ROCAF's air combat capabilities are distributed across five fighter wings, one Flight Training Wing (FTW) and one Combined Wing (CW) situated across seven air bases around the island.

Two Tactical Fighter Wings (TFWs) operate the indigenous AIDC F-CK-1C/Ds – the 1st TFW at Tainan Air Base on the southwest coast and the 3rd TFW at Ching Chuan

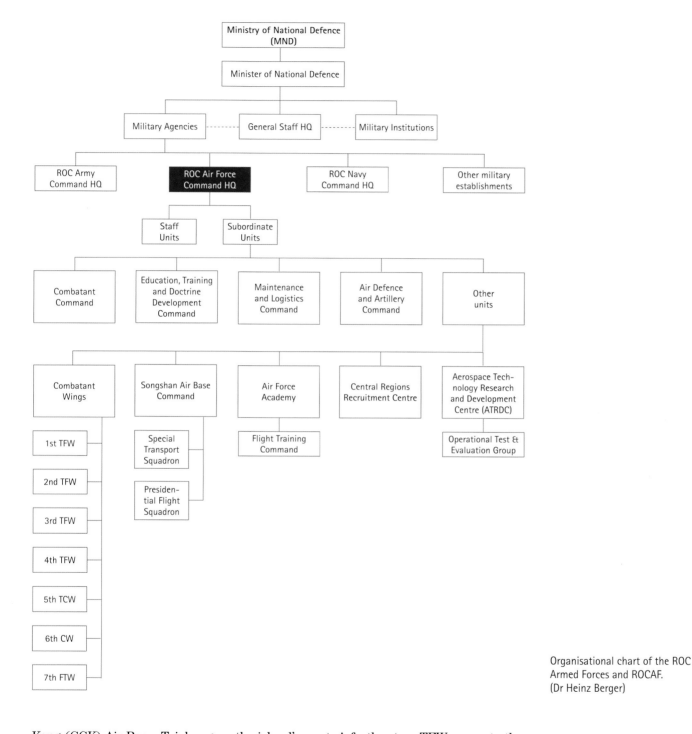

Organisational chart of the ROC
Armed Forces and ROCAF.
(Dr Heinz Berger)

Kang (CCK) Air Base, Taichung on the island's west. A further two TFWs operate the
Lockheed Martin F-16A/Bs and upgraded F-16Vs – the 4th TFW at Chiayi Air Base in
Taiwan's southwest and 5th Tactical Composite Wing (TCW) at Hualien Air Base on the
north-eastern coast. The 4th TFW is currently in the midst of converting to the F-16V
while the 5th TCW will follow shortly. The 5th TCW also fly a handful of photo recon-

naissance-configured Northrop RF-5Es alongside an even smaller number of twin-seat F-5Fs. The 2nd TFW at Hsinchu Air Base on the north-western coast is the sole wing that operates the Dassault Mirage 2000-5DI/EI.

Located on the south-eastern coast, the 7th FTW at Chihhang Air Base, Taitung conducts the lead-in fighter training program with the F-5E/Fs. The 6th CW, which flies a hybrid fleet that includes the Lockheed C-130H, P-3C and Northrop Grumman E-2K, is stationed across Pingtung North and Pingtung South Air Bases on the island's south. Both air bases have their own aerodrome facilities but are linked by a taxiway.

The Songshan Air Base Command at Taipei Songshan Airport is a wing-level unit that operates an administrative transport fleet that comprises the Beech 1900C, Fokker 50 and the Presidential Boeing 737-800. In addition, the Air Force Academy – located at Gangshan Air Base in the southern city of Kaohsiung – flies a trainer fleet made up of the Beechcraft T-34C and AIDC AT-3.

No flying units are assigned to the Chiashan Air Base complex in Hualien although squadron detachments operate from there during exercises and training events. Chiashan is connected to Hualien Air Base via a 1.43 miles (2.3km) taxiway. Magong Air Base, located on Taiwan's outlying islands of Penghu, hosts the Tian Ju (Sky Horse) detachments between April and September annually.

Apart from Chiashan and Chihhang, which were designed and built from the ground up for ROCAF use, all other bases were originally established in the 1930s during Japanese occupation of Taiwan. A number of the ROCAF air bases – Chiayi, Ching Chuan Kang, Hualien and Tainan – are joint-use airports and receive regular civilian and commercial traffic.

Aviation training[1]

The Air Force Academy oversees training and education for all prospective pilots. There are three established pathways to become an ROCAF pilot: a four-year program at the academy; selected top-performing graduates from the Air Force Institute of Technology; and university graduates. The majority of pilot cadets begin their air force journey at the Air Force Academy.

Entrance to the academy is based on high school results. There are four general streams a cadet can specialise in: aerospace engineering; avionics engineering; aeronautical-mechanical engineering and aviation management. To prepare them for the rigours of flight training, physical training is a regular activity in the academy. Upon graduation, they are commissioned as second lieutenants.

Just prior to graduating from the academy, the cadets would have been subjected to a medical examination. Those not found suitable at any stage of the selection program will be reassigned to receive specialised training in subjects such as aircraft maintenance, communications and air warfare before posting to a unit.

The newly commissioned ROCAF officers selected for flight training will then undergo 40 hours of aviation physiology education to familiarise themselves with the physiological hazards associated with flight. Activities conducted at the Aviation Physiology Research Laboratory in Kaohsiung Armed Forces General Hospital include ejection seat training, hypoxia training in an altitude chamber and centrifuge training.

This will be followed by aircrew water survival and jungle survival training, each spanning one week.

Trainees begin their flight training on the Beechcraft T-34 at the Basic Training Section at Gangshan Air Base. All forms of basic and advanced training are conducted here, making this a busy base. Spanning 26 weeks, the basic training program aims to develop the fundamental flying knowledge and skills prior to progressing onto advanced flight training. The program consists of 140 hours of ground school followed by 90 flight hours in 83 sorties. Simulators are also used during the program.

Upon completion of basic training, trainees are streamed to either the Fighter Training Section or the Airlift Training Section. The majority of them are assigned to the former where they will fly the AIDC AT-3. Those on the airlift training track will learn their trade on the Beech 1900.

The advanced training program on the AT-3 is six months in duration, offering trainees 120 hours of ground training and 110 hours of flying training in 85 sorties. Forty-three simulator rides are also carried out. The training aims to instill the fundamentals of jet-flying and prepare ROCAF trainees for the subsequent lead-in fighter training.

With the completion of advanced training on the AT-3, the prospective fighter pilots move to Chihhang Air Base to begin lead-in fighter training on the F-5E/F. In 100 flying hours on the platform, the program introduces trainees to fast-jet operations, exposes them to tactics training and prepare them for transitional training to the F-16, Mirage 2000 and F-CK-1 at the respective operational conversion units.

Both the AT-3 and F-5E/F are programmed for replacement by the AIDC T-5 in the years ahead. This will see the current three-stage fighter pilot training system reduced to two.

ROCAF training syllabus

Training programmes	Aircraft type	Programme duration (weeks)	Flight time (hours)
Basic training	T-34	26	90
Advanced training	AT-3	26–28	110
Lead-in fighter training	F-5E/F	36	100
Airlift training	Beech 1900C	About 6 months	Not known

* Programme duration could vary between students.

Combat wings

The organisation and structure of the ROCAF wings and subordinate units have evolved over time. In the early years of the ROCAF's establishment in Taiwan, the 'wing ⟶ group ⟶ squadron' organisational structure was adopted. The wings were assigned single-digit numbers (1st, 2nd etc.) though the groups were actually the more prominent of the organisation structure. In 1976, to align with the numbering convention used by the army brigades and the navy flotillas, all wings were reassigned three-digit numbers [the first digit of the sum of these numbers would be the previous number of the wing: 443rd (ex 1st) 499th (ex 2nd) etc.].

The 1990s saw a wave of restructuring within the ROCAF. While it anticipated the delivery of its second-generation of fighters, squadrons and a wing were disbanded as the ROCAF gradually drew down the F-5 and F-104 fleets. The Eastern Region Command was set up at Hualien Air Base in 1991 in lieu of the 828th TFW when the latter was stood down. The Taoyuan Air Base Command at the now defunct Taoyuan Air Base was also established in 1998 as a wing-level organisation to oversee the F-5E/F and RF-5E squadrons when the 401st TCW relocated to Hualien.

The final command structure we are familiar today was put in place in 2004. It saw most wings reformed without the intermediate groups while the squadrons were elevated to that of a group: wing ⟶ group. The Tactical Fighter Group (TFG) designation was largely a cosmetic change with each still assigned a complement of about 20 aircraft, though a colonel now heads the unit. A one-star major general commands each TFW.

The designation change was not made to the units of the 737th FTW and the 439th CW likely because of the training function of the former and the latter's diversified fleet and roles. As part of an effort to honour its roots, the ROCAF decided to revert its wings back to single-digit numbers in December 2017.

ROCAF combat wing designations before and after Dec 2017

Prior to December 2017	After December 2017
443rd TFW	1st TFW
499th TFW	2nd TFW
427th TFW	3rd TFW
455th TFW	4th TFW
401st TCW	5th TCW
439th CW	6th CW
737th FTW	7th FTW

An eighth combat wing, the 828th TFW, was established at Hualien in 1982 with the F-5A/B, subsequently converting to the F-5E/F. The wing stood down in 1992.

As an example for a ROCAF wing, the following section details the history of the 5th TCW.

5th Tactical Composite Wing[2]

The F-5s and F-16s of the 5th TCW are among the most recognisable ROCAF aircraft. The tail of every assigned aircraft is adorned with a distinctive sun motif to pay homage to the aboriginal Amis tribe, who worshiped the sun god Malataw. The artwork was designed by then commander of the wing Major General Pan Gong-xiao and was gradually applied across the fleet from 2004.

The wing can trace its roots to the 5th Pursuit Group (later Fighter Group), which was established in 1936 at Jianqiao, Hangzhou in China just one year before the Second Sino-Japanese War. The group was assigned to Zhijiang, Hunan Province to join the Chinese-American Composite Wing when it was activated in 1943 with the P-40 Warhawk. While greatly outnumbered, the group's pilots clocked up over 120 kills

A number of 5th TCW F-16A/Bs received high-visibility sun motifs in the 2000s, but these were gradually toned down over the years. The last aircraft to carry the colourful tail flash was F-16A tail no. 6677 – assigned to the commanding officer of 26th TFG. This was removed when he was killed in a crash in November 2020.
(Peter Ho)

against Japanese aircraft. Towards the end of the Chinese Civil War in 1948, the group was moved across the straits to Taoyuan Air Base from its last mainland base in Nanjing.

The 5th Fighter Group was upgraded to wing status in 1953 and converted to the North American F-86F Sabre two years later. During skirmishes with the PLA Air Force between 1955 and 1958, the wing claimed 24 Chinese MiG kills and was awarded the honorary Tiger Banner by President Chiang Kai-shek for the outstanding achievement.

Due to the different aircraft the wing operated, it was designated a Tactical Composite Wing in 1960. The wing transitioned to the Northrop F-5A/Bs in 1968. In 1976, it was re-numbered the 401st TCW and re-equipped with the F-5E/F in 1978. It began training on the F-16A/B in 1997 shortly after deliveries to Taiwan were made. The 401st TCW moved to Hualien Air Base in July 1998 with the 8th Group moving the other way to Taoyuan. One reason for the move was due to lobbying by former members of the wing to avoid diminishing its rich heritage should it be assigned under the Taoyuan Air Base Command. In 1999, the 401st TCW received its first F-16A/Bs. Former President Chen Shui-bian visited the base on 16 January 2002 to mark the wing's successful conversion to the type.

In December 2017, the wing reverted to its 5th TCW designation. It is due to receive upgraded F-16Vs once sufficient aircraft have populated the other F-16 wing – the 4th TFW.

Currently, the 5th TCW includes the following four TFGs:

12th Tactical Reconnaissance Group
The 12th TRG 'Tigergazer' has always been at the forefront of the ROCAF's reconnaissance efforts and is famed for the stories of its daring photo-reconnaissance flights over Chinese territory to monitor military developments. In the 1950s it operated the RF-86F and the Republic RF-84F from Taoyuan, before converting to the Lockheed RF-104G in the 1960s.

The squadron also briefly flew the McDonnell Douglas RF-101 when its sister reconnaissance squadron, the 4th Tactical Reconnaissance Squadron (TRS) 'Red Fox' was stood down in 1973. In the 1980s, it flew the AIDC R-CH-1 (a reconnaissance variant of the T-CH-1 Chung Hsing – a local copy of the T-28 Trojan) alongside Shi'an RF-104Gs. In 1992, the squadron moved from Taoyuan to Hsinchu so as to receive better maintenance support from the F-104-equipped 499th TFW. After acquiring RF-5Es modified by Singapore Aerospace in 1997, it retired the last of the F-104s the following year.

Just one year after operations with the RF-5E, the Tigergazers relinquished the type to the 4th TRS which had re-established in Taoyuan. In 2002, the unit was formally inaugurated under the 401st TFW at Hualien with the F-16 and subsequently obtained the Phoenix Eye LOROP pods. In 2005, the 4th TRS once again disbanded as a squadron and was subsumed as a flight under the 'Tigergazers'. Some of the RF-5Es feature a 'Red Fox' marking on the forward fuselage for this reason. Today, 12th TRG continues operating both types as the sole ROCAF photo-reconnaissance unit.

17th Tactical Fighter Group
While the 17th TFS has been established under the 5th TFG since 1936, insufficient F-5A/Bs for the wing led to reassignment to the 2nd TFW at Hsinchu in 1971, flying F-100s. It returned to Taoyuan in 1974 and re-equipped with the F-5A/B. The squadron

operated F-5E/Fs from 1978 till 1998 when it moved to Hualien. In March 1999, the unit was commissioned as the first F-16A/B squadron under the 401st TFW.

The 17th TFG is the ROCAF's dedicated aggressor unit. It took on the role in 2002 in-lieu of the Chihhang-based 46th Squadron, which had relinquished its 'red air' assignment prior to 2000. Its warfare tactics instructors – who have mostly received training in the United States – are not only expected to be well-versed with the F-16 but also adversary tactics. Replicating 'red air' profiles against their operational brethren, the instructors teach the nature of these threats and pass on lessons vital for survival in air combat.

The 'Thunder' Group also conducts the Joint Warfare Tactics Course for ROCAF officers. The goal of the program is to strengthen joint warfighting skills and produce tactical experts in the exploitation of air, land, sea and cyber capabilities.

26th and 27th Tactical Fighter Groups
The 26th TFS 'Witch' and the 27th TFS 'Black Dragon' traded in their F-86Fs for the F-5A/B in 1968 and completed conversion by 1970. The 27th TFS also took on hand a number of the 28 Northrop T-38A Talons loaned by the United States in 1972, in exchange for the transfer of Taiwan's F-5As to the South Vietnam Air Force. Both units were declared operational with the F-5E/F in 1978. After moving to Hualien in 1998, both units began converting to the F-16A/B.

The 26th and 27th TFGs are tasked with the anti-shipping mission with the AGM-84L Harpoon missile. As the traditional F-16 operational conversion unit – the Chiayi-based 21st TFG – has transitioned to the F-16V, the 27th TFG has also been temporarily allocated the F-16A/B type-conversion role as of December 2020.

Fighter alert and defence coverage

With the ever-present threat from across the straits, fighter units of the ROCAF are arguably among the world's busiest and at the highest readiness. Fighters with CAP loadouts are commonly seen launching and recovering at air bases. Alert duties are rotated between the TFWs and TFGs. A high readiness team at different TFWs could stand alert at the same time to allow better coverage of different sectors.

Furthermore, the 1st and 3rd TFWs each contribute a three-month rotation of F-CK-1s for the six-month long Tian Ju mission between April and September at Magong. Only the F-CK-1s – which number between 12 to 20 aircraft per detachment – are allocated this mission due to the ability to launch within five minutes, among other operational considerations; it takes an extra minute to scramble the F-16 and Mirage 2000. The forward deployment is conducted in the spring and summer months as weather and winds conditions are less favourable for flight operations at other times of the year. Located at just 31 miles (50km) from the median line – a demarcation drawn down the centre of the Taiwan Strait by the United States in the 1950s but never agreed upon by the Chinese – the forward deployment allows scrambling fighters a quicker transit time to intercept encroaching PLA aircraft.

However, its proximity to the frontline means that the mission is only viable during peace time as PLA firepower would be brought to bear on the facility at the start of an all-out war.

During combat operations, air force doctrine divides the airspace into three tiers: high, mid and low altitude levels. The high-tier is from 35,000 feet (10,668m) and above, the mid-tier from 20,000 to 35,000 feet while the low-tier is below 20,000 feet (6,096m). ROCAF fighters are assigned to the defence of each tier based on capability and performance attributes as well as operational considerations.

The F-CK-1's poorer endurance and lack of engine thrust at higher altitudes have generally relegated the type to lower-level defence. On the other hand, the French fighter's superb acceleration and time-to-altitude profile makes it ideal for high-altitude intercept missions. Strategically based at Hsinchu to cover the air protection of the important political and economic centres in northern Taiwan, the Mirage 2000s could climb at speed to an advantageous height and position to employ its MICA BVR air-to-air missiles against enemy aircraft above the strait.

C4ISR[3]

Taiwan's development of its command, control, communications, computers, intelligence, surveillance and reconnaissance (C4ISR) infrastructure was spurred by the revolution in military affairs (RMA) following the display of the Chinese military threat in the strait crisis of 1995–1996.

The FPS-115 Pave Paws, established atop the Leshan mountain under the Surveillance Radar program. It allows not only long-range surveillance deep into Chinese airspace, but also vital early warning of missile attacks.
(Peter Ho)

Radar sensors

The principal air surveillance network of the ROCAF comprises 14 radar units – broken down into seven squadrons, six sections and one centre-level organisation – situated around Taiwan's coastal areas and offshore islands. These units operate both fixed and mobile radars that are believed to include: seven fixed Lockheed Martin AN/FPS-117s, four TPS-77s – mobile-versions of the FPS-117, two fixed Raytheon HR-3000s, one fixed Lockheed Martin GE-592 and two mobile Northrop Grumman AN/TPS-75s. The mobile radars, used in concert with the ROCAF's six E-2K Hawkeyes AEW aircraft, provide not only gap-filler coverage but also greater survivability of air surveillance. If required, the ROC Navy's four *Keelung*-class (former *Kidd*-class) destroyers could also provide additional redundancy with its SPS-48E 3D air search radar.

Taiwan's most capable and imposing radar system, however, would be the Raytheon AN/FPS-115 Pave Paws – a long-range early warning radar that has its roots in the Cold War. Completed at a cost of USD 1.38 billion in 2013 under the Surveillance Radar Program (SRP), the system is made up of a transmitter building with two phased array antennas built atop the Leshan mountain near Hsinchu's Wufeng Township. Located at an elevation of 8,530 feet (2,600m), the system has a reported maximum range of 3,100 miles (5,000km) though some sources indicate that the United States might have this curtailed by a third or more. This would still allow a coverage area that spans the Korean peninsula to the northern parts of Southeast Asia, though line-of-sight limitations would require a target to be at high altitudes at the further end of these ranges.

The Leshan radar station is reported to be able to track as many as 1,000 aircraft and ballistic missile targets simultaneously and provides more than six minutes warning in the event of a missile attack. The system's constant surveillance deep into Chinese airspace would have been equally useful during peacetime, yielding significant intelligence on Chinese airpower and missile developments in the last decade. The presence of United States personnel at the radar station has been widely reported and even captured in official photographs, although MND has been quick to pass them off as technical advisors. Plans to purchase a second radar system, which would have been built in the south near Kaohsiung, was reportedly abandoned in 2007.

These sensors feed an air situation picture to the Joint Air Operations Centre (JAOC), the ROCAF's principal body tasked with the continuous monitoring of Taiwan's airspace and the orchestration of air and GBAD assets against intruders. The facility is buried within a hill known as Chanchu Shan (Toad Mountain) and accessible from Fuxing Camp in southern Taipei. The command and control (C^2) functions of the JAOC are supplemented by three publicised Regional Operations Control Centres (ROCCs) located in the north – Taipei Zhongshan District, south – Kaohsiung Qishan District and east – Hualien Xincheng Township. The ROCCs provide additional back-up capacity for the ROCAF's tactical air defence command and control. Other facilities like the Chiashan Air Base mountain complex could also function as additional layers of redundancy.

Datalink[4]

Forming the backbone of the ROC armed forces' C4ISR system architecture is the Hsun'an (Quick and Secure) system, or sometimes known by its program name Bo Sheng (Broad Victory). Through the adoption of a mix of Link 16 Joint Tactical Information Distribution System (JTIDS) and Multifunctional Information Distribution

System – Low Volume Terminals (MIDS-LVT), a number of Taiwan military's sensors, weapon systems and C^2 centres are integrated to form a 'system of systems'. This enables seamless dissemination of operational information and the sharing of a common tactical picture with friendly assets.

According to Taipei-based defence analyst Kitsch Liao, the encryption hardware for the Bo-Sheng program was primarily of US origin, supplemented by ones developed by the National Security Bureau (NSB) – Taiwan's principal intelligence agency.

The Bo Sheng program has not been without its challenges. Conceived in the late 1990s, it was intended to integrate then standalone C^2 networks of the three services. With an initial price tag of USD 4 billion, budgetary constraints forced the program to be split into two phases. Between 2004 to 2009, the first phase of Bo-Sheng equipped Link-16 terminals on around 36 F-16s, six E-2s, a number of ROC Navy ships and a few theatre-level ROC Army commands. Integration of F-CK-1 was not considered for the first phase of the project, while the planned integration of 20 Mirage 2000s did not proceed due to technical difficulties and the French's unwillingness to provide relevant data.

The second stage of the program was subsequently cancelled due to phase one falling below expectations, primarily due to technical, organisational and bureaucratic issues, according to Liao. The rest of the F-16 fleet was progressively linked to the network, which was then officially termed the Hsun'an system.

Liao said, '*Significant challenges remain for ROCAF, since the Mirage 2000-5s are unlikely to be integrated into Hsun'an, while upgrading the F-CK-1s with the data links was deemed too expensive. Either a work-around allowing these two fleets to exchange digital information with the existing network, or a significant redesign of force structure would be required.*'

Force preservation

The Central Mountain Range, the peaks of some of which rise to almost 13,000 feet (3,962m), divides Taiwan into eastern and western sectors. This has led to a situation where air bases could only be built in the flat regions along the east and west coast.

The ROCAF's ability to continually generate its airpower from these bases throughout a military conflict will be a key factor in Taiwan's ability to defend itself. Aircraft on the ground are mere targets. They only become weapons of war when they are airborne, sufficiently fuelled and armed with the right mix of munitions. China is acutely aware of this vulnerability and would ensure they will be taken out at the start of hostilities.

Hardening[5]
Alongside active defences such as GBADs, Taiwan has employed passive defence measures to counter the PLA's missile and air attacks. Since the 1950s, Taiwan has utilised ingenious underground hardened complexes to protect its military forces, as exemplified by tunnels and strongholds built in the frontline islands of Kinmen and Matsu, many demilitarised and open to the public. The effort to bury and harden the ROC military has grown since then. The most important of this is the Joint Operations Command Center, otherwise known as the Hengshan Command Centre that was built into a mountain in the Taipei suburb of Dazhi. Completed in 1982 after 22 years of

construction, the facility is a tri-service C^2 centre for the highest-level of the military and the president.

The ROCAF also has an established doctrine emphasising dispersal and hardening to ensure survivability. Taiwan has built two sanctuaries on its east coast to shelter its fighter aircraft from attacks. These are the Chiashan (Optimal Mountain) base in Hualien and the smaller Shizishan (Stone Mountain) facility at Chihhang Air Base in Taitung.

Both hardened bases were conceptualised in the early 1980s under Project Jian'an (Build Safe), with some literature calling the Chiashan facility the Project 828 and the Shizishan facility the Project 737, taking on the number designations of the fighter wings then assigned to the base. It has been reported that a seven-men engineering team visited a number of European countries in 1981 to learn the New Austrian Tunnelling Method (NATM) in excavation works.

The ambitious construction of Chiashan began in 1984 and took eight years to complete, costing nearly USD 1 billion. The project hollowed out a granite mountain in the Hualien mountain ranges some 1.86 miles (3km) west of Hualien Air Base. Surrounded by the Central Mountain Range and only with its eastern flank exposed, Chiashan was thought to be invulnerable to any attacks from the air when conceived.

Media reports over the years have discussed about its ability to hold up to 200 fighters, underground power generators, medical facilities, C^2 infrastructure and several

Mirage 2000-5EI tail no. 2032 awaits its next sortie at a hardened shelter at Hsinchu Air Base.
(Stephan de Brujin)

months' supply of food and fuel. Analysis of satellite images reveal eight taxiways leading out from the mountains to a 1.5 miles (2.4km)-long runway. Individuals who have visited the base have spoken of massive steel blast doors at the entrances that could withstand the shock of a potential hit. According to them, the base comprises a northern and southern complex, each made up of five horizontal and five vertical tunnels interlaced together in a criss-crossed fashion. The taxiway tunnels reach up to a height of about three stories.

Speculation that fighters housed in the caverns could initiate their take-off runs from within is inaccurate due not only to safety reasons but also insufficient airflow in the tunnels for such an operation. In fact, early speculation points to there being inadequate exhaust ventilation in the caverns for an aircraft to start their engines for taxi. As such, a departing aircraft would have to be towed out to the entrances. It is not known if such a design flaw, if true, has been resolved.

Chihhang's Shizishan is a smaller facility built at the north-eastern corner of the air base. Compared to Chiashan's caverns, observers have likened it to a rabbit warren that could house approximately 80 fighters.

Should the cross-strait situation becomes tense, the ROCAF intends to evacuate the main portion of its fleet to the two hardened bases. Exercises are regularly conducted with unit detachments operating from these facilities. The ROC military's largest annual wargames Han Kuang (Han Glory) would typically see a detachment of fighters deploying to Chiashan on the first day of the week-long exercise.

Separately, most of the 250 or so hardened aircraft shelters in use today date back to the 1970s and would not be able to withstand a direct hit from modern munitions. As such, the ROCAF has embarked on the construction of its next generation hardened shelters under Project Jian'an VI. Thirty-six protective shelters, designed to take the direct impact of a 2,000lb (907kg) bomb, are being built at CCK Air Base over a seven-year period from 2020 at a cost of USD 157 million. It is expected that new hardened aircraft shelters will also be built at Chihhang Air Base, which has been identified to receive new F-16C/Ds from 2023.

Dispersion

The ROCAF maintains five acknowledged highway sites located in the vicinity of air bases that can be converted to dispersal sites should the need arise. Four are located along No 1 National Freeway, which spans 233 miles (375km) along the west coast connecting Taiwan's northern tip in Keelung to the southwest corner in Kaohsiung. These are the Changhua section (near CCK), Minxiong section (near Chiayi), Rende as well as Madou sections (near Tainan). A fifth is located on the Jiadong section of Provincial Highway 1 (near Pingtung). These sections were built in the 1970s with combat utility in mind – as many as eight sections were planned for airstrip operations. The freeway tracts completed for this purpose are around 9,843ft (3,000m) in length and 131ft (40m) wide, designed with a weight-bearing capacity of at least 100 tons and a full cement base with a thickness of 15.75in (40cm). To facilitate quick conversion to an airstrip, minimal highway lightings are installed and the concrete median dividers could be easily removed.

Highway drills are the highlight in the Han Kuang exercises when they are held, though they are not commonly organised due to the traffic disruptions. Eight have been conducted since the first in 1975; the next was scheduled at the Jiadong section in July 2021. A typical format of the exercise would see single examples of the ROCAF fighters and an E-2K Hawkeye landing on the strip, backtracking to a refuelling and rearming point and then launching with a full weapon load.

Recovery[6]

The quick recovery of air bases following enemy attacks will also be key to sustain the air force's operability. The ROCAF is known to have capable rapid runway repair (RRR) teams trained to quickly make assessments of the damage and conduct repair operations following an attack. A period of about 90 to 120 minutes is often suggested as a duration an ROCAF RRR team would take to bring a damaged runway to operational status, though this would largely depend on the damage inflicted and if unexploded ordnance is still among the rubble.

The ROCAF is also believed to possess a sizable fleet of armoured repair vehicles and runway repair kits deployed at its main air bases. One known repair kit system in use by the ROCAF was purchased from Rapid Mat U.S., Inc. in 2002. Taiwan's RRR capability has also benefited from engineering exchanges with the USAF. ROCAF delegates are regularly dispatched to the USAF-hosted the annual Silver Flag exercise in which airfield damage repair is one of the focuses. USAF combat engineering and explosive ordnance disposal (EOD) teams have also visited Taiwan to train with the ROCAF.

Concealment

Lastly, Taiwan also utilises concealment and deception in hopes of reducing the effectiveness of the targeting of its air bases. Camouflage, both natural and artificial, are used to conceal and confuse the enemy while decommissioned aircraft – primarily F-5Es – are placed around air bases to deceive attackers in wasting their munitions on non-targets. With the advent of high-resolution satellite imaging systems, this would probably be less effective today.

ROCAF F-16V, Mirage 2000-5DI, F-CK-1D and E-2K aircraft are fuelled and rearmed during a highway drill along the Changhua section of the No. 1 National Freeway during the Han Kuang exercise in May 2019.
(Military News Agency)

Ground-based air defence[7]

On 1 September 2017, the ROCAF inaugurated the Air Defence and Artillery Command, combining its Air Defence Command and the Air Defence Missile Command which had previously been under the purview of the MND's General Staff Headquarters. The restructure unified the control of air defence under the ROCAF, thereby streamlining the chain of command. Air defence coverage for deployed forces in the field remain with the ROC Army and Marine Corps.

The ROCAF operates a multi-layer integrated air defence system with a variety of systems that provide overlapping coverage and complementary capabilities to handle different threats. For ballistic missile defences, it has the Raytheon Patriot Advanced Capability 2 (PAC-2) and PAC-3 systems. The PAC-2 missiles have been upgraded and incorporated within the PAC-3 batteries such that firing units of both types can be often seen deploying together in exercises. It was announced in March 2021 that Taiwan intends to purchase the PAC-3 Missile Segment Enhancement (MSE) interceptors for delivery from 2025.

Taiwan has also produced an indigenous SAM system – the Tien Kung (TK) Sky Bow system – with technical assistance from the United States. Manufactured by the defence ministry's research and development agency – National Chung-Shan Institute of Science and Technology (NCSIST), three versions have been developed since the initiation of the project in 1979.

The earliest, the TK-1, remains in service and are deployed in both vertical-launched cells at missiles silo bases and mobile trailer launchers. With an engagement range of 63 miles (100km), the TK-1s are only useful against aircraft.

The TK-2, which entered service in 1997, has double the range of the TK-1. While initially fielded in missile silo facilities, recent evidence points to the TK-2 being operationally deployed on mobile launchers, too. Although still not effective against ballistic missiles, it can be utilised in defending against cruise missiles.

The latest version, the TK-3, entered service in the mid-2010s after a lengthy period of development and evaluation that began in the late 1990s. Also reported to have a range of 125 miles (200km), the TK-3 is a full-fledged anti-ballistic missile (ABM) system. A series of missile tests in 2020 at Jiu Peng Missile Range in Taiwan's southeast has ignited speculation of an extended-range, high-altitude version of the TK-3 with interception capabilities not dissimilar to that of the United States' Terminal High Altitude Area Defense (THAAD) system.

Since the mid-1990s, the TK missile systems have been deployed on the outer islands of Dongyin and Penghu, putting Chinese aircraft launching from air bases in Fujian Province within its coverage, assuming they have not been destroyed by missiles and artillery fire during the onset of war.

With the PAC-2, PAC-3 and TK-3 systems combined, the ROCAF has about 1,000 anti-ballistic missile interceptors. This is still significantly below the 1,200 to 1,500 SRBMs that the PLA Rocket Force (PLARF) has in its arsenal against Taiwan, particularly when two or more interceptors would be ripple-fired against a single SRBM target.

The ROCAF has also confirmed in November 2020 that its Raytheon MIM-23 HAWK missile batteries have been re-tasked to defend against lower altitude targets after being superseded by the TK-3. The HAWK's system AN/MPQ-50 Pulse Acquisition

Radar has been replaced with the NCSIST-developed CS/MPQ-90 Bee Eye active electronically scanned array radar, which has a range of about 25 miles (40km).

For the air protection of bases and point defence, the ROCAF utilises the wheeled vehicle-mounted Jie Ling (Antelope) short-range air defence system, which employs four NCSIST Tien Chien (Sky Sword) I missiles. Separately, the ROCAF operates the Skyguard air defence system in a unique configuration. The system pairs the Oerlikon GDF-006 35mm guns, upgraded to fire Advanced Hit Efficiency and Destruction (AHEAD) munitions, together with Raytheon RIM-7 Sparrow missiles.

Several of the ROC military's radar stations have emplaced Phalanx close-in weapon systems (CIWS) repurposed from decommissioned ROC Navy ships to counter anti-radiation and cruise missiles. Under Project Tian Sun II (Sky Falcon II), the ROCAF had plans to purchase additional Phalanx systems for deployment at Chiashan and Shizishan bases but now appears to favour an indigenous solution by NCSIST.

The ROCAF air defence network system – known as Huan Wang – aggregates information from radar stations and SAM sites to the JAOC, prioritising targets according to the nearest engagement system available. According to defence analyst Kitsch Liao, the system is linked to the ROC military's Hsun'an system but is not integrated with Patriot and TK-3 batteries. This is being remedied in an ongoing program.

Raytheon Patriot PAC-2 and PAC-3 firing units provide air defence coverage during a highway drill. Acquired in 1997, the PAC-2 missiles have been upgraded and incorporated as part of PAC-3 systems, which were purchased in the late 2000s.
(Roy Choo)

Ground-based offensive missiles[8]

Indigenously developed by NCSIST, Taiwan's surface-to-surface missile systems are shrouded in secrecy and are subjected to much speculation by the local media. Due to their sensitive nature, the MND does not comment on the capability, though hints have been periodically dropped by defence officials and indications in government budgetary documents have signalled of their existence. It is understood that the missile systems are under the responsibility of the ROCAF's Air Defence and Artillery Command.

The possession of the offensive missiles broadens the counterstrike options for Taiwan in the event of a potential PLA missile attack and Chinese invasion. Used in concert with other ROCAF air-launched stand-off munitions, Taiwan hopes the ability to reach out and strike PLA missile launchers, air and naval bases, C^2 nodes and impose damage on other Chinese economic and state targets, would deter China from launching actual attacks.

The United States has traditionally been against the deployment of such weapons by Taiwan, stressing the destabilising nature of such systems. The approval of the AGM-84H Standoff Land Attack Missiles (SLAM-ER) and MGM-140 Army Tactical Missile System (ATACMS) by the Trump administration could herald a new direction in United States policy but with the change of administration this is now not certain.

According to media sources, Taiwan commenced the development of such offensive systems soon after the 1995–96 Taiwan Strait crisis when it realised that it did not have the means to retaliate against a Chinese missile attack.

The TK-2 surface-to-air missile system was modified and lengthened to produce a SRBM. Most reports have named the missile the TK-2B, with a stated range of 310 miles (500km).

The Hsiung Feng (HF)-2E [Brave Wing 2E] is a land attack cruise missile system that has received much coverage by the media over the years. Adapted from the HF-2 subsonic anti-ship missile, it is believed to have entered service in late 2000s. With an indicated range of 373 miles (600km) – the whole of Fujian – the closest Chinese province to Taiwan, parts of Zhejiang and Guangdong are within reach of the missiles if fired from the Penghu islands.

Budgetary statements in 2011 have alluded to the basing of the HF-2Es on the Penghu archipelago. The HF-2E missiles are reportedly fired from truck-mounted launchers and possibly fixed silos.

Citing an unidentified source in the military, Taiwan media reported on 11 January 2021 that the long-rumoured 745 miles (1,200km) extended-range version of the HF-2E has been delivered to the ROCAF. If true, major cities such as Shanghai and naval bases at Qingdao and Hainan Island are now within striking distance of the ROC military.

Yet another offensive system that is widely reported is the Yun Feng (Cloud Peak) cruise missile. Even less is known about this system, which first surfaced in the media around 2012.

Media outlets have discussed tests of the Yun Feng over the years and have spoken of an earlier 745 miles (1,200km) range version and an extended-range variant of 1,243 miles (2,000km).

ORBAT of the Republic of China Air Force

Order of battle of the Republic of China Air Force (ROCAF) as of April 2021

Air Base (Unit/Squadron)	Location	Aircraft type	Remarks
ROCAF Command HQ			Taipei
Combatant Command	Taipei		
Education, Training and Doctrine Development Command	Chiashan AB (Hualien)		
Maintenance and Logistics Command	Taipei		
Air Defence and Artillery Command	Tainan		
Tainan Air Base			Tainan
1st Tactical Fighter Wing			
1st Tactical Fighter Group 'Gymnogyps'	Tainan	F-CK-1C, F-CK-1D	Operational conversion unit
3rd Tactical Fighter Group 'Celestial Eagle'	Tainan	F-CK-1C, F-CK-1D	
9th Tactical Fighter Group 'Bugs Bunny'	Tainan	F-CK-1C, F-CK-1D	
Hsinchu Air Base			Hsinchu
2nd Tactical Fighter Wing			
41st Tactical Fighter Group	Hsinchu	Mirage 2000-5DI, Mirage 2000-5EI	
42nd Tactical Fighter Group 'Cobra'	Hsinchu	Mirage 2000-5DI, Mirage 2000-5EI	
48th Training Group	Hsinchu	Mirage 2000-5DI, Mirage 2000-5EI	Operational conversion unit
Ching Chuan Kang Air Base			Taichung
3rd Tactical Fighter Wing			
7th Tactical Fighter Group 'Coyote'	Ching Chuan Kang	F-CK-1C, F-CK-1D	
28th Tactical Fighter Group 'Baby Dragon'	Ching Chuan Kang	F-CK-1C, F-CK-1D	
Aerospace Technology Research and Development Centre (ATRDC)			
Operational Test & Evaluation Group	Ching Chuan Kang		Aircraft loaned from units as required
Aerospace Industrial Development Corporation (AIDC)	Ching Chuan Kang	XT-5	Two flying and two static prototypes undergoing testing
Chiayi Air Base			Chiayi
4th Tactical Fighter Wing			
21st Tactical Fighter Group 'Gamblers'	Chiayi	F-16A Block 20, F-16B Block 20, F-16V Block 20	F-16V operational conversion unit; in process of converting from F-16A/B to F-16V

22nd Tactical Fighter Group 'Condor'	Chiayi	F-16A Block 20, F-16B Block 20 F-16V Block 20	In process of converting from F-16A/B to F-16V
23rd Tactical Fighter Group 'Tzu Chiang'	Chiayi	F-16A Block 20, F-16B Block 20, F-16V Block 20	In process of converting from F-16A/B to F-16V
Air Rescue Group 'Seagull'	Chiayi	EC225, S-70C-6, UH-60M	Search and rescue, with detachments in Chihhang and Songshan
Hualien Air Base			Hualien
5th Tactical Composite Wing			
12th Tactical Reconnaissance Group 'Tigergazer'	Hualien	RF-5E, F-5F, F-16A Block 20, F-16B Block 20	Reconnaissance role
17th Tactical Fighter Group 'Thunder'	Hualien	F-16A Block 20, F-16B Block 20	Aggressor training role; due to receive F-16V
26th Tactical Fighter Group 'Witch'	Hualien	F-16A Block 20, F-16B Block 20	Due to receive F-16V
27th Tactical Fighter Group 'Black Dragon'	Hualien	F-16A Block 20, F-16B Block 20	F-16A/B OCU; due to receive F-16V
Pingtung North Air Base			Pingtung
6th Combined Wing			
Anti-Submarine Warfare Group	Pingtung		
33rd Squadron	Pingtung	P-3C	
34th Squadron 'Black Bat'	Pingtung	P-3C	
20th Electronic Warfare Group	Pingtung		
2nd Early Warning Squadron	Pingtung	E-2K	
Pingtung South Air Base			Pingtung
6th Combined Wing			
10th Tactical Airlift Group 'Camel'	Pingtung		
101st Airlift Squadron 'Cattle'	Pingtung	C-130H	
102nd Airlift Squadron 'Horse'	Pingtung	C-130H	
20th Electronic Warfare Group	Pingtung		
6th Electronic Warfare Squadron	Pingtung	C-130HE, C-130H	
Chihhang Air Base			Taitung
7th Flight Training Wing			
7th Flight Training Group			
44th Flight Training Squadron	Chihhang	F-5E, F-5F	
45th Flight Training Squadron 'Black Panther'	Chihhang	F-5E, F-5F	
46th Flight Training Squadron 'Aggressors'	Chihhang	F-5E, F-5F	

Gangshan Air Base			Kaohsiung
Air Force Academy			
Flight Training Command			
Basic Training Section	Gangshan	T-34C-1	
Fighter Training Section	Gangshan	AT-3	
Airlift Training Section	Gangshan	BH-1900C-1	Aircraft loaned from Special Transport Squadron
Instructors Training Section	Gangshan	AT-3, T-34C-1	
Aerobatic Team 'Thunder Tiger'	Gangshan	AT-3	Active during display season

Songshan Air Base Command			
Special Transport Squadron	Songshan	BH-1900C-1, EBH-1900C-1, Fokker 50	
Presidential Flight Squadron	Songshan	Boeing 737-800	

Magong Air Base			Magong, Penghu
	Magong	F-CK-1C, F-CK-1D	1st and 3rd TFWs each contribute 3-month rotational Tian Ju (Sky Horse) detachments between April and September annually; in 2021, due to heightened tensions, this has been extended to a full year

Overseas Locations			
Luke AFB			Arizona, USA
56th Fighter Wing 'Thunderbolts'			
21st Fighter Squadron 'Gamblers'	Luke	F-16A, F-16B	ROCAF F-16A/B training detachment; expected to move to Tucson, AZ
Edwards AFB			California, USA
412th Test Wing			
416th Flight Test Squadron	Edwards	F-16V	USAF flight test unit with ROCAF F-16Vs embedded

C² infrastructure
I. JAOC
II. Leshan Radar Station

Air bases
1. Tainan (1st TFW)
2. Hsinchu (2nd TFW)
3. Ching Chuan Kang (3rd TFW)
4. Chiayi (4th TFW)
5. Hualien (5th TCW)
6. Pingtung North (6th CW)
7. Pingtung South (6th CW)
8. Chihhang (7th FTW)
9. Magong
10. Chiashan
11. Gangshan

Key
⊕ Air base
◉ C² infrastructure
● City
— Motorway
— Major road

▶ A physical map of Taiwan showing the air bases and the Taiwan Strait median line. (Map by James Lawrence)

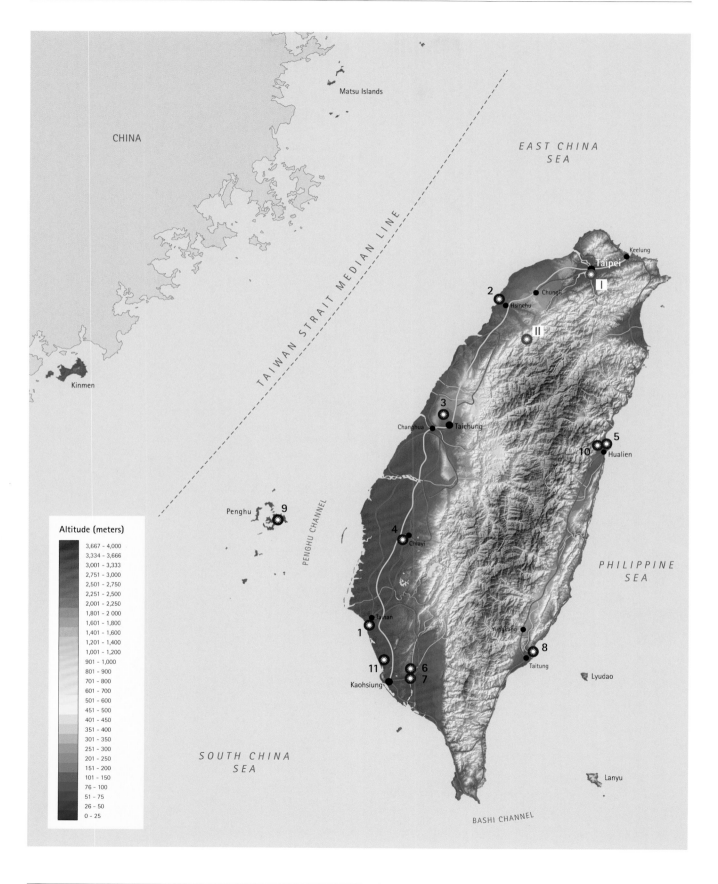

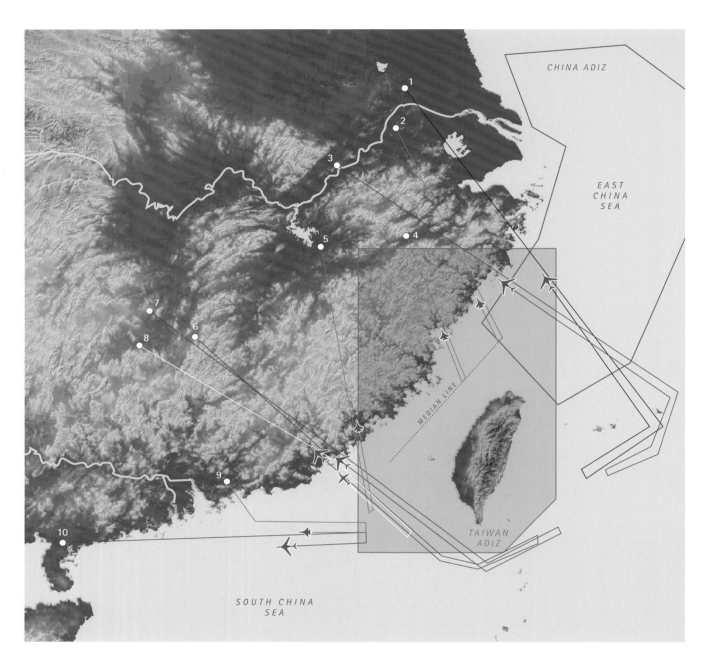

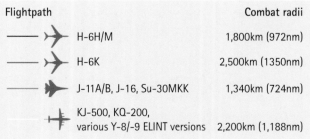

Flightpath		Combat radii		PLA air bases ETC		PLA air bases STC
✈	H-6H/M	1,800km (972nm)	○	1. Luhe/Ma'an	○	6. Leiyang
✈	H-6K	2,500km (1350nm)		2. Wuhu		7. Shaodong
✈	J-11A/B, J-16, Su-30MKK	1,340km (724nm)		3. Anqing North		8. Linling
✈	KJ-500, KQ-200, various Y-8/-9 ELINT versions	2,200km (1,188nm)		4. Quzhou		9. Huiyang
				5. Nanchang Xiangtang		10. Suixi

AIRPOWER AND STRATEGY OVER THE TAIWAN STRAITS

Roy Choo

China's military modernisation has proceeded with impressive speed. In a span of less than two decades, the balance of power around the Taiwan Strait has swung irreversibly in its favour. It has not been afraid to employ coercive airpower operations against Taiwan to show where the island stands in the new strategic landscape. Taiwan has struggled to rejuvenate its air force and is increasingly under strain as it stands on heightened alert to respond to every Chinese incursion into its airspace.

In this chapter, we assess the threats to the ROCAF, the evolution of its airpower strategy and how the ROCAF would likely function in a war scenario. We also take a look at the role the United States plays in Taiwan's airpower and also the development of its indigenous defence effort.

The geopolitics of Taiwan[1]

The strategic significance of Taiwan lies in its pivotal location off the China coast and between Northeast and Southeast Asia. During World War II, Taiwan was used by Japan as a launch pad for its air raids on both Philippines and Indonesia. It was also a key logistics hub to sustain the Japanese war effort in China and throughout Southeast Asia. During the Vietnam War, Taiwan was utilised as a critical staging point for United States cargo and troop airlift flights as well as aerial refuelling tankers and fighter aircraft.

Seventy years after the end of the Chinese Civil War as we know it, the PRC sees Taiwan as a breakaway province that will eventually be reunited as part of the country. The crux of this claim goes beyond the usual rhetoric of nationalism.

Integrating Taiwan into the PRC would strengthen China's strategic position, allowing it to assert its maritime and territorial claims, including what it terms the 'nine-dash line', a vast area in the South China Sea. China also believes that in order to secure its sea borders and avoid containment by the United States, it needs to control and break through the 'first island chain', which runs from Kamchatka to Borneo and includes Taiwan. Gaining control of Taiwan would provide China unrestricted access to both waterways to the island's north and south – Miyako Strait and Bashi Channel respectively. This would enable China to project air and naval power further out of the first island chain and threaten United States forces coming from Hawaii and the West Coast, thereby shifting the regional balance of power in the Western Pacific.

◀ Taiwan's official ADIZ, demarcated in the 1950s, overlaps with China's ADIZ and even partially covers the mainland. As the administering of such a zone is impractical, actual enforcement is conducted in a significantly smaller airspace.
The red dragon's claws: this map shows a few examples of known flight paths noted during 2019-2021 and most likely ones from the major bases responsible for coercive air operations against Taiwan.
(Map by James Lawrence)

Second, Taiwan is an economic power in its own right and a major investor in the world economy. It is a critical node in the global technology supply chain and is home to many local and foreign technology companies. Bringing Taiwan's economy into its fold would be advantageous for China.

Third, Taiwan's vibrant democracy at its doorstep has proven to be a bone in Beijing's throat and undermine the CCP at home. As such, Taiwan's strategic importance to China from a military, economic and political standpoint are evident.

The issue of the security of Taiwan is not concerned merely with Taiwan but also with the stability of the entire Asia-Pacific region. In essence, the ability of the ROC Armed Forces to defend Taiwan – with or without the assistance of the United States armed forces – will have repercussions far wider than the immediate region.

Assessing the PLA threat

The rise of Chinese airpower is well documented and can be read in Harpia's excellent series on the PLA aviation arms. We will, however, analyse the dynamics of the threats that the ROCAF are facing.

Missile strikes[2]
China's investments in its missile programs are largely driven by two key motivations: the rapid and decisive defeat of Taiwan through the destruction of its air bases, while at the same time, the establishment of an anti-access/area denial (A2/AD) envelope primarily around the 'first island chain' to complicate any American intervention.

According to a 2017 paper on China's air base strike capabilities by Oriana Skylar Mastro and Ian Easton from the Project 2049 Institute – a Washington D.C. think tank, the Chinese began the development of dedicated ground and air-launched missiles that could be armed with runway-penetrating sub-munitions in the wake of the 1995-96 Taiwan Strait crisis. Researchers conducted detailed studies on the most effective tactics and techniques to successfully 'blockade an enemy's runway'.

China has gone to great lengths to ensure its missile threats are not hypothetical. In 2006, satellite imagery was discovered of a mock-up of the ROCAF's CCK Air Base 5 miles (8km) east of the PLAAF's Dingxin Air Base in the Gobi Desert. The replica was of the same orientation and exact dimensions of its runway and taxiways. This area is known to be used for missile testing and large craters could be seen around the mock target. Similar mock-ups have also been made of Japanese air bases utilised by the USAF with precise impacts clearly seen on aircraft and hardened shelter targets.

According to most estimates, the PLA Rocket Force (PLARF) fields 1,200 SRBMs and 250 transporter erector launcher (TELs). The SRBMs are of the Dongfeng (DF)-11, DF-15 and DF-16 variety. Unfortunately for Taiwan, it has very limited strategic depth and proximity to the mainland implies that it is within reach of the shortest-range of SRBMs even if fired from deeper inland.

The highly accurate Iranian ballistic missile strikes on the United States military-occupied Al Asad Air Base in Iraq in January 2020 should alleviate any notion that newer SRBMs remain as inaccurate as older Cold War-era models. Using a mix of unitary and submunitions warheads, an entire air base could be put out of action for a while.

Of concern to Taiwan are also the Changjian-10 (CJ-10) - also known as Dongfeng-10 (DF-10) - ground-launched land attack cruise missiles. Additionally the PLAAF's H-6K bombers that conduct 'encirclement flights' around the island are commonly armed with KD-63 LACM but can be equipped with the air-launched version of the missile – known as the KD-20 – to not only demonstrate that Taiwan could now be struck from a variety of directions but also that the ROCAF's Chiashan and Shizishan facilities on the eastern coast are no longer safe.

Taipei-based independent defence analyst Wendell Minnick, who previously had the opportunity to visit the Chiashan Air Base complex, is not optimistic about the survivability of such hardened facilities. Speaking to the author, he said: '*Chiashan was built long before the advent of China's ability to use cruise missile and bunker buster munitions, so it was assumed the facility would be protected. But with China's military capabilities today, such an installation would not last long. The PLA will be able to sustain a multi-dimensional and multi-directional ballistic missile and cruise missile attack against all of ROCAF air bases.*'

Sustained Chinese missile strikes could ultimately overwhelm Taiwan's missile defences and could indeed disable many – if not all – of the runways at Taiwan's major fighter bases. Consistent waves of attacks could undermine any attempts to recover the bases. However, not all targets can be struck with ease from afar; specific scenarios might still see attack aircraft and bombers deployed to prosecutes targets at a closer range.

China's pursuit of hypersonic boost-glide missiles, which has the manoeuvrability and speed far in excess of rocket-powered missiles, will only make the defence against Chinese attacks much harder.

The PLARF's large numbers of SRBMs and cruise missiles, such as the DF-10, present a credible threat to the ROCAF's ability to generate its air power. (China Military/Zhang Feng)

Fighter imbalance[3]

A key finding of any objective analysis of Taiwan's air defence situation must be the disparity in numbers and capability of the ROCAF's front-line fighter aircraft vis-à-vis the PLA.

The PLAAF has been a major beneficiary of the military modernisation effort. During the 1995-1996 crisis, it had just over 24 fourth-generation Sukhoi Su-27s and was, for the most part, a local air defence force. Through leveraging on local developments of the Flanker family and indigenous production of fourth and fifth-generation fighters, the PLAAF is today an all-round modern air force.

The 2020 United States DoD annual report to Congress on PLA developments states the PLAAF and PLA Navy (PLAN) Air Force field a combined fleet of over 800 fourth-generation multi-role fighters – the J-10, J-11, J-16, Su-30 and Su-35 – and a limited number of fifth-generation fighters – the J-20. Aerial refuelling – a capability that the ROCAF lacks, presents a further force multiplier effect for Chinese air power.

With embarked J-15s on the PLAN's two ski-jump operational carriers – the *Liaoning* (16) and *Shandong* (17), the PLA now possesses the ability to project air power towards Taiwan in any direction it wishes. More flat-deck catapult-equipped conventional take-off carriers are expected to be launched in the next decade.

On the other side of the strait, the ROCAF fourth-generation fighter fleet comprises 141 F-16s, 55 Mirage 2000s and 129 F-CK-1s as of December 2020. Mostly delivered in the late 1990s, these fighters were near the limits of their ability to remain competitive by the late 2000s. Fortunately, substantial upgrades began to be rolled out to the fleet from the early 2010s. The F-CK-1s have been put through a decade-long mid-life upgrade while the F-16s began theirs from 2017. Taiwan's urgent requirement for new-built fighters finally made headway when the Trump administration approved the sale of 66 F-16C/D Block 70s in August 2019. Scheduled for delivery from 2023, these would likely go towards the full or partial replacement of a present aircraft type rather than an outright expansion of the fighter fleet.

The substantial cross-strait 'fighter-gap' aside, a comparison will also need to be made on the man behind the machine. The lack of exposure to bilateral and multilateral training curtails our understanding of the training quality of the PLA airmen. However, according to the DoD report, Chinese leaders have continued to place emphasis on the need to build up the PLA combat readiness so that it can 'fight and win'. It added that this entails conducting more realistic and rigorous training and also the addressing of issues in complex joint operations training.

ROCAF pilots, on the other hand, train and operate to established American proficiency standards. Its F-16 pilots in particular, are sent to the United States to undertake advanced training at the 21st Fighter Squadron detachment at Luke AFB and also attend prestigious programs such as the USAF Test Pilot School at Edwards AFB.

The SAM threat[4]

China's SAM systems add an extra threat dimension that the ROCAF combat aircraft would have to contend with. The PLA's formidable area defence missile systems comprise the S-300PMU-2 – received in the 2000s – and the indigenous Hongqi-9 (HQ-9). Units operating these systems are based along the Fujian coast, and with their engagement range of 125 miles (200km), ROCAF aircraft flying over the Taiwan Strait and much of the western coast are under threat.

The PLA's induction of the S-400 system in 2018 has also given its air defence forces a further boost. It is due to receive the 40N6 missiles that would extend its range to 248 miles (400km) range, theoretically placing the whole of Taiwan under its reach. The S-400 will, however, still not be able to engage at all altitudes east of Taiwan as the Central Mountain Range, coupled with the Earth's curvature, would mask aircraft from radar detection. PLA airborne early warning and control (AEW&C) aircraft will be needed to provide targeting data over these regions.

With AEGIS-equivalent ships such as the Type 055 and Type 052D destroyers, the PLAN has also build up an impressive seaborne area defence capability. Equipped with phased-array radars and a sizable load of vertical-launched long-range HaiHongqi-9 (HHQ-9) SAMs, these ships could provide a protective umbrella around an invasion fleet against ROCAF aircraft conducting maritime strike missions.

ROCAF in a war scenario[5]

To better understand how the ROCAF would fight in a conflict with China, we evaluate the air arm in the following scenario based on its known existing capabilities.

An assault on Taiwan would not spring out of the blue. Certain 'red lines' drawn by Beijing would have been crossed. The weeks, and perhaps months, leading up to a conflict would be fraught with aggressive military posturing on both sides, high-profile large-scale exercises and the Chinese's waging of psychological warfare to erode Taiwan's willpower. Actual low-intensity conflict, such as the seizing of Taiwan's offshore islands – Dongsha and Taiping Islands in the South China Sea for example – would have already occurred.

Taiwan's national defence plan, known as the Gu'an (Solid and Secure) Operational Plan, would also be put into action. Little is known about the Gu'an plan, but according to Ian Easton in his book on the Chinese invasion threat, it is thought to be a detailed playbook for the defence against all acts of Chinese aggression, including a full-scale invasion. The plan is constantly revised when new intelligence is available on the PLA or when new capabilities are received by Taiwanese forces.

Under the Gu'an directives, ROC military reservists from across all services would have been mobilised in large numbers to undergo refresher training and fortify the island's defences. The ROCAF would go through a force preservation phase, which would entail the evacuation of a large portion of its fighter fleet to the Chiashan and Shizishan hardened facilities, as discussed in Chapter 2 of this book. Depending on the how tight the timelines are, the evacuation effort would be a logistical challenge, requiring massive manpower and equipment transportation that would not be fulfilled by the 19 ROCAF C-130H transport fleet alone. A token fighter force might still be left behind in their home bases to provide an all-round air defence coverage and to allow for increased survivability through dispersing of operations. To that end, detachments of fighters and E-2Ks could also deploy out to converted highway strips and civilian airports to further complicate PLA targeting.

Taiwan will also be expected to place emergency orders with the United States for critical supplies of munitions just as it was reported to have done during Taiwan Strait missile crisis in March 1996; the order was cancelled after the crisis ended. The present ROCAF air-to-air missile inventory is insufficient to counter the vast PLA air fleet. In particular need would be AIM-120 AMRAAMs, which number between 300-400. For a fleet of 141 F-16s, this would furnish a ratio of just over two missiles per aircraft. Production of locally produced Tien Chien missiles will be similarly stepped up.

The start of the PLA's Taiwan campaign would envisage what many Chinese scholars term the dian xue zhan (acupuncture war) – a term for the quick decapitation of an enemy with precision strikes at pressure points and nodes. For this, PLARF SRBMs will be launched at the ROC military's eyes and ears – radars and sensors, bases and any force that could mount a resistance. ROCAF ballistic missile and air defences will be deployed at the ready to thin down the numbers though it will be inevitable that many will get through due to their sheer volume. By this stage, a blockade of Taiwan would have been put in place by the PLA, which the ROC forces will resist.

ROCAF fighters that have been airborne in CAPs before the initial wave of missile strikes will engage in aerial engagements with PLA fighters, most of these at beyond-visual range. These would soon be joined by fighters from bases that remain functioning post-attack. Runway-repair teams will endeavour to get cratered runways back to operational status to enable more fighters to join in the fight. Loses in the air will be suffered on both sides but the quantitative advantage of the PLA would give it an edge.

Taking advantage of breaks between waves of missile attacks, ROCAF fighters with stand-off air-launched munitions will attempt to destroy SRBM TELs and cruise missile launcher vehicles as they proceed to replenish their missile loads. PLA bases, air and naval bases will also not escape unscathed as Taiwanese fighters and ground-launched missile forces strike at these facilities in attempts to blunt the PLA war-fighting capability.

In an unthinkable scenario in which the PLA is determined to bring Taiwan under Chinese control, a fleet of PLAN ships comprising Type 075 and Type 071 amphibious ships – under the protection of destroyers and frigates – will be used to transport an invasion force across the strait. By this time, the ROC military will be under severe attrition from the relentless missile and air attacks. In collaboration with ROC Navy warships and submarines, surviving ROCAF F-16s would conduct anti-ship missions with AGM-65G and AGM-84L Harpoon missiles while warding off PLA fighters and SAMs.

According to some analysts, rather than outright Normandy-style beach landings which will result in significant casualties, the bulk of the PLA invasion force would likely arrive at captured Taiwanese sea ports. Further troop reinforcements from the air could be brought in by PLAAF transport aircraft at captured airports. ROC Army and Marine Corps forces will lead the resistance on the ground against the PLA thrust while ROCAF fighters will conduct interdiction missions in support of the effort.

Taiwanese military officials have publicly admitted that the armed forces could hold out unassisted for at least two weeks in the hope that the United States or the international community would come to its aid.

Grey-zone warfare[6]

Of more concern today, however, is China's 'grey-zone' assault on Taiwan. This refers to operations by a state actor that fall below the threshold of a military conflict but could still erode a foe's will to resist through exhaustion. China has progressively stepped up

A 5th TCW F-16A, 6663, intercepts a PLAAF H-6K during one of the 'island encirclement' drills that have been conducted since November 2016. (MND)

its military coercion against Taiwan since President Tsai Ing-wen, a candidate from an independence-leaning party, took office in 2016.

In November that year, the PLA launched the first of many 'island encirclement' drills with H-6 bombers and escort aircraft. Based on information available, these sorties circumnavigate the island but either do not enter or simply fly close to border of Taiwan's Air Defence Identification Zone (ADIZ) while transiting through the Bashi Channel. Such flights have been conducted intermittently since then and the ROCAF has had most of them shadowed. These sorties are believed to not only serve as open-sea, long-distance training flights for PLA bomber crew but also as a form of psychological intimidation of Taiwan.

Historically, the PLAAF has mostly kept its flights close to mainland shores due not only to the ROCAF's superior capabilities but also to avoid possible defections across the strait. The first known attempts to cross the median line in recent decades took place during the Strait Crisis of 1995-96.

Isolated episodes of intrusions have taken place over the years when Beijing wanted to send a political message, such as when then President Lee Teng-hui declared in July 1999 that a special state-to state relationship existed between China and Taiwan. In July 2011, a pair of J-11s crossed the centreline briefly in a bid to intercept a USAF U-2 reconnaissance aircraft. Another known incursion was made by PLAAF J-11s in March 2019 days after President Tsai made a stopover in Hawaii.

2020 saw a significant escalation in Chinese military coercions. Throughout the year, the PLA made repeated intrusions across both the centreline and Taiwan's ADIZ, in what seemed like an endeavour to push the limits and normalise such flights. The most severe of these occurred on 18 and 19 September in response to a visit by United States Under Secretary of State Keith Krach. In a massive show of force over the two days, four H-6 bombers, 20 J-16s, six J-11s, six J-10s and one KQ-200 anti-submarine warfare aircraft either crossed the centreline or intruded into the southwest corner of the ADIZ. Over the rest of the year and into 2021, PLA KQ-200s made near-daily intrusions into the same corner of the air defence zone, possibly to conduct patrols of the waterway leading to its important naval base on Hainan island (see map on page 36).

The PLA incursions have taken a huge toll on the ROCAF. Former Minister of National Defense Yen Teh-fa on 7 October 2020 told Taiwan's legislature that for the first 10 months of the year, the ROCAF scrambled 2,972 sorties (an unbelievably high number that would likely include combat air patrols and training sorties) to shadow or intercept PLA aircraft, of which 1,710 had intruded into Taiwan's ADIZ. It was subsequently stated that the number of incursions in 2020 had been highest since the 1995-96 crisis. In response to the coercion, the ROCAF F-CK-1 Tian Ju detachment at Magong was extended beyond its usual September conclusion and into 2021 to allow quicker interceptions of PLA aircraft. Taiwan's MND revealed that the scrambles alone had cost the island almost USD 900 million in 2020 and that maintenance costs of its fighters had risen by USD 17 million year-on-year.

Without firing a shot, these daily ROCAF scrambles are gradually wearing out its aircraft and exhausting its airmen. With the PLA in possession of over 4,000 aircraft, it could inflict disproportionate stress on Taiwan's much smaller force of 300 fighters. It seems that the in-service life of the ROCAF fighter fleet is now almost a decision that lies with Beijing.

Of concern are also the incursions in the southwest corner of the ADIZ. Taking place far from the mainland, reaction times by ROCAF will be slower while a constant fighter presence over this area would require even more resources due to the ROCAF's lack of aerial tankers. As a substitute, ROCAF P-3C Orions on maritime patrol duties have been diverted to perform interception tasks. Collin Koh, a research fellow at the S. Rajaratnam School of International Studies in Singapore said: '*The use of P-3C to respond to PLA incursions is symptomatic of Taiwan's capacity shortfalls and brings into question the sustainability of its response measures against PLA forays. The knowledge of the ROCAF's use of these planes for interception missions reflects a sense of desperation – which plays into the hands of Beijing. Overall, it is definitely not the most sustainable way forward.*'

Evolution of Taiwan's airpower strategy[7]

Up till the 1990s, the ROC Army was the dominant force in the military. It was viewed that a strong army would provide the utmost deterrent and that its strength would not allow a PLA invading force to prevail. As such, army-centric military thinking was the guiding principle for Taiwan's defence planning.

During those years, Taiwan's defence posture was based on the principles of 'checking the enemy on his shore; striking the enemy in transit; and annihilating the enemy

on the beachhead'. Thus, the role that the ROCAF was expected to play was that of advanced warning, early attrition and to fight for local air superiority in order to safeguard the ROC Army's operations in 'annihilating the enemy on the beachhead'. Essentially in these army-centric air operational concepts, the ROCAF was regarded as the ROC Army's deterrence multiplier and a semi-independent flying artillery.

In the 2000s, then newly elected President Chen Shui-bian proposed a new strategy of 'active defence'. By then, the authority of the ROC army had waned, and coupled with the growing influence of the United States through arms sales, the ROCAF was encouraged to review and develop its concept of operations. From the mid-2000s, under the concept of 'active countermeasure', the ROCAF acquired precision stand-off weapon systems in order to establish the military's deep strike capabilities. In was during this period that the HF-2E and Wan Chien (Ten Thousand Swords) cruise missiles were developed.

Since then, Beijing's massive military modernisation effort has yielded technologically advanced armed forces with tremendous firepower. With China outspending Taiwan on defence by a factor of 15, the ROC military will never be able to compete force-on-force in a conventional symmetric defence strategy.

Among the earliest to urge a strategic rethink was William S. Murray's paper 'Revisiting Taiwan's Defence Strategy' in 2008. He proposed that rather than relying on its air power which was unlikely to survive a PLA attack, Taiwan should establish a 'porcupine' strategy with A2/AD weapons such as coastal-defence cruise missiles, multiple-launched rocket systems, naval mines and attack helicopters to destroy an invasion force.

Yet another paper by US think tank RAND Corporation in 2016 suggested that Taiwan should downsize and refocus its fighter force to counter PLA coercive scenarios and build up a well-equipped SAM force as a deterrent.

In what has been an official recognition of the changed strategic landscape, Taiwan has begun putting in place a revolutionary defence approach, which it calls the Overall Defence Concept (ODC). Proposed by then-Chief of the General Staff, Admiral Lee Hsi-ming in 2017, much of the strategy remains unknown, although it is stated to embrace an 'innovative and asymmetric' response to the PLA growing threat. As detailed in the 2019 Taiwan National Defense Report, ODC is based on three central pillars 'force protection; decisive battle in the littorals; and destruction of the enemy at the landing beach'. Essentially it calls for riding out the initial missile and air attacks and the subsequent conduct of force-denial operations on follow-on invading amphibious forces.

Some analysts have criticised Taiwan's procurement of 66 F-16C/Ds in 2019, citing their non-conformity to the asymmetric strategy due to their high cost, requirement of a large vulnerable airbase and its limited utility in an air war with the PLA. However, no conventional force is ever fully asymmetric. It is entirely likely Taiwan is pursuing a capabilities balance – between asymmetric and symmetric – to pose a multi-dimensional threat in peace and war.

The F-16C/D Block 70 advanced capabilities, such as conformal fuel tanks, infrared search and track (IRST) system, advanced electronic warfare suite and increased weapons load, provide a force-multiplier effect which could be considered as a touch of asymmetry in itself. Taiwan's ODC strategy continues to evolve and it appears a sizable fighter fleet will still have its place in the asymmetric approach.

The American factor[8]

Taiwan's relations with the United States have always been intrinsically linked to the cross-strait relationship. Under the 1954 US-Taiwan Mutual Defense Treaty, the United States was legally obligated to defend Taiwan by force. It stood by Taiwan in the two strait crises of the 1950s, having even threatened the use of nuclear weapons – which it had kept on the island.

The United States military presence was at one point nearly 20,000 troops on Taiwan under the US Taiwan Defense Command. Over 6,000 of these were stationed at CCK Air Base, which had sizable USAF KC-135, C-130 and rotating fighter detachments supporting the Vietnam War effort. In exchange for Taiwan's willingness to transfer 48 F-5As – received under a Military Assistance Program – to the South Vietnam Air Force, two squadrons of USAF F-4 Phantoms were stationed at the base between 1972 to 1975.

This all came to an end in 1979 when the United States no longer recognised Taiwan and established relations with the PRC. As a consolation for Taiwan, the US Congress passed the Taiwan Relations Act, which mandates the United States to provide 'defensive' arms so that Taiwan can protect itself. Beijing has since vehemently opposed every attempt by the United States to sell weapons to Taiwan and this continues to be a thorn in Sino-American relations.

After much negotiation, Beijing and Washington issued the 1982 Communiqué (known as the 817 Communique in Taiwan due to it being signed on 17 August) which saw the United States agreeing to reduce arms sales gradually, though it did not set an end date to do so. Just a month later, the US unilaterally transmitted to the Taiwanese leadership what is known as the 'six assurances'. It reaffirms its policy not to set a cut-off date and not to consult China on arms sales.

Throughout the late 1970s and 1980s, however, the United States rebuffed nearly every request by Taiwan to purchase arms, including the F-16 and F-20. It instead resorted to technology transfer – an area not covered by the 1982 Communiqué – to help Taiwan produce its own defence equipment.

The sale of 150 F-16A/Bs in 1992 was a major milestone as it surpassed both the quantity and quality levels set in the 1982 Communiqué. The justification provided by the then George H.W. Bush administration was that the sale was necessary to redress the cross-strait military imbalance.

Apart from isolated sales from European defence companies, such as the Mirage 2000, the United States continues to be Taiwan's predominant supplier. Most of the US defence firms do not have any form of business dealings with Chinese interests and are less susceptible to Chinese pressure, unlike many European companies.

In general, arms packages provided to Taiwan have always been conditioned on the threat posed by the PRC and are designed to not trigger an overreaction from Beijing. Arm sales tend to provide a modest upgrade to existing capabilities or those already under development. As an example, the United States agreed to the sale of the F-16A/B when the first of the indigenous F-CK-1s were being produced. Similarly, sales of the AGM-154 Joint Standoff Weapon (JSOW) in 2017 and AGM-84H SLAM-ER in 2020 were approved by the US after the Wan Chien (Ten Thousand Swords) cruise missiles have entered service.

The calibrated approach to arms sales would no doubt also have taken into account the significant number of senior Taiwan military officers caught with espionage involving China. Among the highest-profile case was Major General Lo Hsien-che, who was caught passing classified information on the Bo-Sheng data link program to Chinese agents in 2011.

Nonetheless, recent years has seen an uptick in weapon approvals to Taiwan, signalling stronger support for Taiwan diplomatically and militarily as geo-strategic tensions between China and the United States increase. The Obama administration approved USD 14 billion worth of weaponry to Taiwan between 2009 to 2017, including a mid-life upgrade of the ROCAF's F-16A/Bs. This was more than all previous administrations combined since 1978. In just four years, the Trump administration sold a record USD 15 billion in arms comprising new F-16C/D Block 70s and MQ-9B Sea Guardian drones.

With Washington's policy of 'strategic ambiguity', it remains to be seen if the United States would commit its military to the defence of the island in an actual conflict. However, the US-China great power competition has so far been a boost for Taiwan's airpower development.

Indigenous defence effort[9]

There are two Taiwanese enterprises at the forefront of the island's aerospace and defence industry, both of which can be considered prime contractors in their own right. The first is the National Chung-Shan Institute of Science and Technology (NCSIST) – a state research and development agency not too dissimilar to the United States DoD's DARPA but with its own production capability. The other is the Aerospace Industrial Development Corporation (AIDC), a government-linked company with an extensive track record of aircraft manufacturing and parts fabrication. Both of these enterprises have pooled their strengths together in joint projects; at one time between 1983 and 1996, AIDC was a sub-unit of NCSIST.

Taiwan's inability to purchase the weapons it desired in the late 1970s brought about a focus on self-reliance in defence production. Prior to then, the defence industry of Taiwan was mostly engaged in licenced production or the reverse-engineering of foreign designs.

Taiwan's indigenous defence effort in the 1980s was underscored by what was termed the san dan yi ji (three missiles, one aircraft) – the Tien Chien air-to-air missile, the Tien Kung surface-to-air missiles, the Hsiung Feng anti-ship missile and the F-CK-1 fighter. These programs were important in both the nurturing of national expertise to research and develop cutting-edge defence technologies, often with the support of US technical assistance, and also the management of large-scale projects.

From the 1990s, foreign-produced arms became available once again, and with the lack of local projects to stimulate local talent, Taiwan's defence industry faced a decline. Over a dozen AIDC production engineers who were involved in the F-CK-1 program were known to have been headhunted by Korea Aerospace Industries for its T-50 Golden Eagle and KT-1 Woongbi trainer projects as well as the licenced production of the F-15K Slam Eagle.

President Tsai Ing-wen's government, which came to power in 2016, set a renewed focus on indigenous defence development. Within a year of the administration taking office, the development of the AIDC T-5 advanced/lead-in trainer was approved, rejecting a leading foreign contender– the Leonardo M-346. Also in the works by NCSIST are a range of missiles, drones and other weapons systems deemed crucial to the island's defence.

The latest push for local development is part of a two-pronged 'high-low' mix strategy to strengthen Taiwan's military capabilities. Its indigenous projects tend to suffer from protracted development and local production output is usually insufficient to meet its requirements. Through the fielding of rigorously tested and often battle-proven American arms, augmented with similar types of indigenous equipment, Taiwan hopes to build up a capability over a shorter duration and to complicate China's defence planning with weapons of differing capabilities and performance. The ongoing development of the NCSIST Teng Yun unmanned aerial vehicle (UAV) and the purchase of four MQ-9B UAVs in November 2020 illustrates an example of this strategy.

Compared to most air forces, the ROCAF has been slow in subcontracting labour-intensive non-essential functions to commercial entities. At present, only a small portion of its maintenance, repair and overhaul (MRO) work is done by contracted companies. These include ground support provided by AIDC for AT-3s and overhaul work by MRO company Air Asia for its C-130, Fokker 50 and Beech 1900 fleets.

In December 2019, AIDC and Lockheed Martin signed a strategic collaboration agreement to establish Taiwan as the first Asia-Pacific maintenance centre for the F-16. The centre, located in AIDC's Taichung Shalu complex where F-16V upgrade work is also conducted, was initially billed as a servicing hub for not only the ROCAF's sizable F-16 fleet but also those of regional air force. The latter would have been near impossible without the client nation incurring the wrath of China.

Positioning the Shalu complex for F-16 MRO work makes commercial sense as the ROCAF F-16V upgrade progresses towards completion and both capacity and manpower are gradually freed. On the unveiling of the centre in August 2020, AIDC President Ma Wan-june said that the company was focussing on producing and repairing F-16 components for the time being. In January 2021, AIDC and the ROCAF signed a five-year contract worth USD 83.3 million to support the maintenance of F-16s.

Since 2000, AIDC has been contracted to provide target-towing services in support of air gunnery exercises by ROCAF fighters. Modified ROCAF F-5Es were used for this task till 2018 when F-CK-1Cs took over the assignment.

AIRCRAFT OF THE ROCAF

Roy Choo and *Peter Ho*

ROCAF tail number system

The ROCAF utilises a four-digit tail number system for its aircraft. The numbering convention is structured around the aircraft type, aircraft variant (if any) and individual aircraft number. There could be exceptions to this system if a group of numbers have been used by an aircraft type previously or if the quantity of aircraft to be inducted into service is over a hundred, resulting in a conflict with another number group.

ROCAF Air Rescue Group UH-60M Black Hawks, which were transferred from the ROC Army, are currently the only aircraft with three-digit tail numbers.

The ROCAF aircraft tail numbers are not to be confused with serial numbers which are featured on the tails of a few of the aircraft types. ROCAF F-5s carry USAF serial numbers while the F-CK-1s and AT-3s have AIDC production serial numbers.

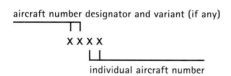

aircraft number designator and variant (if any)

X X X X

individual aircraft number

ROCAF number scheme.

Tail no. range	Aircraft type and variant	Tail no. range	Aircraft type and variant
0801 to 0863	AT-3	3301 to 3315	P-3C
931 to 945	UH-60M	3401 to 3444	T-34C
1301 to 1320	C-130H	3701	Boeing 737-800
1351	C-130HE	5001 to 5003	Fokker 50
1401 to 1504	F-CK-1C	5101 to 5342	F-5E
1601 to 1629	F-CK-1D	5351 to 5416	F-5F
1901 to 1912	Beech 1900C	5501 to 5507	RF-5E
2001 to 2048	Mirage 2000-5EI	6601 to 6720	F-16A
2051 to 2062	Mirage 2000-5DI	6801 to 6830	F-16B
2251 to 2253	EC225	7015 to 7018	S-70C-6
2501 to 2506	E-2K		

Lockheed Martin F-16A/B Block 20 Fighting Falcon[1]

Background

Taiwan had expressed interest to purchase the F-16 as soon as it became available for export in the 1970s. However, the United States' switch in recognition from the ROC to the PRC in 1979, followed by the signing of the 1982 Communiqué, made the sale of the fighter – even the substantially downgraded F-16/79 – all but impossible.

In a sharp reversal to this policy, President George H.W. Bush, who was on his re-election campaign, announced in September 1992 the sale to Taiwan of 150 F-16A/Bs, broken down into 120 single-seaters and 30 twin-seaters. Although his main thrust was that the F-16s were necessary to boost Taiwan's defensive capabilities, the 1989 Tiananmen Square Incident and France's willingness to sell Mirage 2000s to the island had made the climate conducive for the sale. Worth nearly USD 6 billion, the Peace Fenghuang (Phoenix) Foreign Military Sales (FMS) program was signed two months later.

Handover of the F-16A/Bs began in mid-1996, these going to the reactivated 21st Tactical Fighter Squadron under the 56th Fighter Wing at Luke AFB, Arizona. Prior to the delivery, the initial cadre of pilots trained on F-16C/D Block 42s with the 162nd Fighter Wing at the Tucson Air National Guard (ANG) Base, also in Arizona.

The first two aircraft to be brought home – F-16A 6609 and F-16B 6810 – were flown from Fort Worth, Texas to Chiayi Air Base on 14 April 1997. The nine-day journey saw stopovers in Hickam AFB, Hawaii and Andersen AFB in Guam. Tanker support was provided by American KC-10s – the only time these aircraft were refuelled mid-air. At the controls were two USAF pilots, with ROCAF Lieutenant Colonel Hao Guang-ming in the backseat of the twin-seater. The aircraft and subsequent deliveries went to the 455th TFW (today's 4th TFW), with the 21st TFS (later the 21st TFG) 'Gamblers' being the first of its three units to convert to the aircraft from F-5E/Fs. A fourth unit, the 14th TFS was transferred to the wing from where it had been based in Hualien in July 1998 to provide additional operational conversion capacity. The unit stood down in October 2004 once its mission was fulfilled. The 455th TFW was declared the ROCAF's first operational wing in December 2001. The second wing, the 401st TCW (today's 5th TCW), was commissioned at Hualien Air Base in January 2002.

The ROCAF commemorated 20 years of F-16 operations in April 2017. There have been nine attrition loses over the years, including one in the United States. The most recent one occurred on the evening of 17 November 2020 when Hualien-based F-16A 6672 was lost along with the commanding officer of 26th TFG.

Of the surviving 141 aircraft, 126 are based in Taiwan and 15 are stationed in the United States. Two of these, F-16A 6601 and F-16B 6801, are attached to the USAF 416th Flight Test Squadron at Edwards AFB for test and evaluation work in support the ROCAF F-16 fleet. They were extensively test-flown as the pattern aircraft for the Taiwan F-16V mid-life upgrade program. The remaining 13 aircraft are assigned to the 21st FS. Due to sensitivity, all ROCAF US-based F-16s carry only USAF insignia and markings. In contrast, another partner nation F-16 squadron at Luke – the Singaporean 425th FS – fly with a mix of its own national and USAF markings.

Over the last 25 years, scores of ROCAF F-16 pilots have walked through the doors of the 21st FS. As a way to pay homage to its roots, the squadron identifies itself as the 'Gamblers', in step with the Chiayi's 21st TFG. The unit is an important conduit for the sharing of USAF tactics, techniques and procedures (TTPs) with the ROCAF.

F-16A tail no. 6660 configured for a typical combat air patrol mission, armed with AIM-9M Sidewinder and AIM-120 AMRAAM missiles. (Peter Ho)

Taking advantage of large open tracts of airspace, a number of advanced courses are conducted here, such as the fighter tactics improvement training and advanced tactical air combat. The duration of these courses varies between one to six months for the intermediate to advanced courses. These are supported by a team of USAF instructors who are also augmented by a handful of ROCAF instructors on a two-year tour. Maintenance and engineering support of the 21st FS F-16s are provided by civilian contractors.

It was announced in 2018 that the 21st FS would relocate to Tucson ANG Base the following year to make room for USAF and international partners' F-35s at Luke AFB, though this had not taken place by early 2021 and could have been delayed indefinitely.

Description

Although Taiwan's preference was for the F-16C/D, which had already superseded the A/B variant on Lockheed Martin's Fort Worth production line, the United States was only willing to supply the F-16A/B Block 20, a model unique to Taiwan.

The Block 20 was however far more advanced than earlier A/B models. Utilising the Block 15 OCU (Operational Capability Upgrade) as the baseline, it incorporates wings of the Block 40, tail of the Block 50 and avionics comparable to the European mid-life upgrade program. Similar to the European F-16AM/BMs, the cockpit features two multi-function displays. The Block 20s utilise the Northrop Grumman APG-66(V3) radar, similar to the V2 model but with the continuous-wave illumination function for the AIM-7 Sparrow missile. The aircraft are powered by the more reliable Pratt & Whitney F100-PW-220 engine.

Weapons and stores

Initially delivered with just AIM-9M Sidewinder and AIM-7M Sparrow missiles, the F-16A/Bs have had their capability increased by incremental sales of weapons and equipment. Between 1998 to 2001, items approved for sale by the United States government included AGM-84G Harpoon anti-ship missiles, AGM-65G Maverick air-to-ground missiles as well as AAQ-19 Sharpshooter targeting pods and AAQ-20 Pathfinder navigation pods – downgraded versions of the LATIRN system.

Perhaps the most important air combat capability upgrade for the ROCAF F-16A/B was the sale of 200 AIM-120C missiles in 2000 – although only 120 were ordered. According to the terms of the sale, these were to be stationed in Guam and only transferred to Taiwan when the PLA acquired a similar active radar homing air-to-air missile, like the Russian R-77 (AA-12), or if actual hostilities broke out. The Chinese testing of the R-77 in June 2002 sped up the delivery; the first batch of AIM-120C-5 AMRAAMs were received by November 2003. One other sale of 218 AIM-120C-7s was approved in 2007.

F-16s of the 4th TFW at Chiayi are assigned the air-to-ground role using an assortment of munitions. These include the AGM-65B TV-guided and AGM-65G infrared-guided air-to-ground missile, as well as the 500lb GBU-12 and 2000lb GBU-10 Paveway II laser-guided bombs (LGB). Pathfinder and Sharpshooter pods are exclusively used

The AGM-84 Harpoon capability on ROCAF's F-16s provides a key element of the ROC military's ability to defend its waters. (Peter Ho)

F-16B tail no. 6825 from the 5th TCW carries a load of TV-guided AGM-65B Maverick anti-surface missiles. These missiles are less often seen on Hualien-based F-16s, since the 4th TFW at Chiayi is assigned the air-to-ground role. (Peter Ho)

by the wing to facilitate the employment of LGBs. The F-16s were used operationally for the first time on 27 October 2005 when two Chiayi-based aircraft dropped four GBU-10s on a Benzene-carrying South Korean chemical cargo ship, the *Samho Brother*. The ship had capsized following a collision but remained upright in the waters off Taoyuan. Results were dismal and the mission was considered a failure – only one bomb scored a hit and the ship remained afloat post-attack.

Meanwhile, the anti-ship mission is entrusted to the 26th and 27th TFGs of Hualien's 5th TCW. The ROCAF is in possession of about 110 AGM-84L air-launched Harpoon II missiles. A batch of 60 missiles and 50 upgrade kits for the earlier AGM-84G were procured in 2007. The pairing of F-16 and AGM-84 Harpoon is a key element in Taiwan's ability to defend important strategic waterways. On many occasions that PLAN aircraft carriers transited the Taiwan Strait, the Hualien-based F-16s would launch combat air patrols with live Harpoons.

For intelligence, surveillance and reconnaissance (ISR) and battle damage assessment (BDA), the 12th TRG of the 5th TCW employs the AN/VDS-5 LOROP reconnaissance pod. Ten of the pods were understood to have been procured in the late 1990s and early 2000s under Project Feng Yan (Phoenix Eye), as the system is more commonly known. The system is thought to be based on the Tactical Airborne Reconnaissance Pod System (TARPS) used by the F-14 and features KS-87B camera, KA-99A panoramic camera, and AN/AAD-5 infrared camera. The set-up is housed in a Modular Reconnaissance Pod manufactured by Danish company Per Udsen (now Terma).

Images are digitally captured, and while they were intended to be transmitted real-time to a ground station, there are some indications this is not carried out due to some unspecified difficulties. With a coverage range of about 58 miles (94km), a Phoenix Eye pod-equipped F-16 flying on its side of the Taiwan Strait, could conduct photo-reconnaissance on targets up to 19 miles (30km) within Chinese territory on a clear day. Aside from providing imagery intelligence that could aid decision-making by field commanders during combat operations, the Phoenix Eye system has been put to good use over a number of peacetime missions. F-16s with the pods have been used to conduct reconnaissance on Chinese carriers when they pass through the straits and also assess damage caused by natural disasters such as typhoons.

According to media reports, the Phoenix Eye system's poor serviceability and less than optimal performance at night has spurred the ROCAF to seek a new pod. An image of the PLAN aircraft carrier *Liaoning* (16) – believed to be taken by a Phoenix Eye pod – in April 2020 was so grainy that that some media commentators wondered if the quality had been deliberately reduced to mislead on its capability and justify the procurement of a new system. In October 2020, the United States government approved a sale of six Collins Aerospace MS-110 LOROP pods for delivery in 2024. Using multi-spectral imaging technologies comprising seven colour channels, the MS-110 offers improved image resolution and coverage in both day and night.

The Phoenix Eye LOROP pod was introduced to service with the 5th TCW's 12th TRG in the early 2000s to provide the F-16 with a photo-reconnaissance capability. The system is starting to show its age and will be replaced by MS-110 LOROP pods from 2024 onwards.
(Peter Ho)

The ROCAF purchased 80 sets of Raytheon AN/ALQ-184 self-protection electronic countermeasures (ECM) pods in 1994 and remains the sole international user today. As part of the F-16 mid-life upgrade, it has sought to either upgrade the pods to incorporate Digital Radio Frequency Memory (DRFM) technology or purchase new AN/ALQ-131A pods with DRFM. As the USAF was pursuing the development of the ALQ-131A, the ROCAF decided to do the same based on a 2012 government-enacted policy to seek commonality with the USAF to ensure cost and maintenance efficiency. In the event, the USAF decided to terminate the ALQ-131A project in 2017. Hence, the ROCAF will continue using the ALQ-184 while it seeks an updated ECM pod solution. Although not commonly seen, the F-16s can also deploy the AN/ALE-50 towed decoy, a system which has been in use since the mid-2000s.

In the coming decade, the F-16 fleet will see further integration of weapons – the majority of these enabled by the mid-life upgrade. Some of the F-16Vs are already starting to carry AIM-9X Sidewinders. Other weapons that could follow, as announced under multiple FMS notifications, include AGM-84H SLAM-ER, AGM-88 High-Speed Anti-Radiation (HARM) missiles, AGM-154 JSOW, CBU-105 Sensor Fused Weapons, GBU-31/38 Joint Direct Attack Munitions (JDAMs) and GBU-54/56 Laser JDAM.

Approved by the United States State Department in separate deals in 2017 and 2020, the HARM, JSOW and SLAM-ER weapons will offer the F-16 an offensive punch that would have been inconceivable when the platform was purchased. With a range of 170 miles (270km) – more than a quarter longer than the indigenous Wan Chien –

A 455th TFW (today's 4th TFW) F-16A configured with inert AIM-9M Sidewinder and AIM-7M Sparrow missiles as well as AN/ALQ-184 self-protection ECM pod on the belly. The AIM-7 has largely been superseded in service by the AIM-120 AMRAAM. (Peter Ho)

Dramatic condensation clouds form on F-16A tail no. 6609 of 455th TFW (today's 4th TFW) during a 2017 air display at Gangshan Air Base. The aircraft is one of three F-16A/Bs which received tail markings to commemorate the 80th anniversary of the 14 August 1937 aerial victory over Hangzhou, which was achieved by the then 4th Pursuit Group. (Peter Ho)

the SLAM-ER provides greater penetrating power with its 800lb (360kg) warhead. The ROCAF has also been seeking the AGM-158 Joint Air-to-Surface Standoff Missile (JASSM) but has thus far not been successful.

The ROCAF 4th TFW F-16s have also been observed carrying AN/AAQ-33 Sniper Advanced Targeting Pods from February 2021. Two of these were purchased in 2015, probably for test and evaluation work with the Edwards-based F-16s, while a further 18 were ordered in 2018.

Mid-life upgrade

On the back of the United States' continued rebuffing of requests for F-16C/Ds, Taiwan submitted a Letter of Request in November 2009 to upgrade its F-16A/Bs. The program was aimed to upgrade their combat capability, extend their service life and address problems of obsolete spare parts.

In September 2011, United States Congress was notified of an FMS for the ROCAF F-16 upgrade worth an estimated USD 5.3 billion. Apart from some of the weapons mentioned previously, the deal included Active Electronically Scanned Array (AESA) radars, Link 16 tactical data link terminals, new mission computers, Joint Helmet Mounted Cueing Systems (JHMCS) and night vision goggles (NVGs) – which ROCAF pilots are not currently equipped with.

An engineering study was conducted to evaluate the replacement of the F-16A/B's F100-PW-220 engines (23,930lb thrust) with the F100-PW-229 (29,160lb thrust). While possible, the additional cost of USD 1.8 billion was deemed not to be cost-effective as the aircraft were already mid-way through their lifespan.

Known locally as Project Feng Zhan (Phoenix Rising), Taiwan's upgrade program was supposed to tie in with the USAF's F-16 Combat Avionics Programmed Extension Suite (CAPES) program. In October 2012, Lockheed Martin was awarded a USD 1.85 billion contract to perform the upgrade. In line with CAPES, the Northrop Grumman APG-83 Scalable Agile Beam Radar (SABR) was selected in August 2013. The subsequent USAF's defunding of the CAPES in 2014 forced Taiwan to take on additional non-recurring engineering (NRE) costs related to the research, development and testing of the radar.

The project stipulated that Lockheed Martin would upgrade the two ROCAF F-16A/Bs based at Edwards AFB as prototypes while the rest of the conversion work would be done locally by AIDC under contract to Lockheed. The first of the two (93-0702/ROCAF tail no. 6601) flew on 16 October 2015. Delays to software testing had an impact on follow-on upgrade work in Taiwan. The first four F-16s were only inducted into AIDC's Taichung Shalu complex in January 2017.

After more than one and a half years of retrofit work, the initial upgraded F-16 (single seat aircraft no. 6626) was test flown in August 2018 and delivered to the ROCAF two months later. Four aircraft were delivered in 2018, 11 in 2019, around 20 aircraft in 2020, and a further seven aircraft by the first quarter of 2021; all of these were taken on by the 4th TFW at Chiayi.

The project had originally envisaged upgrading a minimum of 24 aircraft per year but issues encountered resulted in significant slippage to the schedule. In a Legislative Yuan (Taiwan's parliament) session in October 2019, the then defence minister Yen Teh-fa attributed the delays to insufficient personnel and expertise at AIDC, compounded by problems with sub-system integration. It was also understood that airframe corrosion and fatigue was found to be greater than what had been expected.

Apart from Taiwan's high humidity climate, the use of the F-16A/B's lightweight landing gear for a heavier airframe in the class of the F-16C/D was believed to be a factor for this issue. Further adding to the complexity of the earlier phase of the program was that the initial aircraft selected for the upgrade already had a multitude of existing technical issues.

Upgraded aircraft are known by AIDC as F-16A/B Block 20 MLU. An official name is yet to be ascertained, though, it is widely referred to by the ROCAF and the media as the F-16V. Through the APG-83 SABR, the detection and engagement ranges of the ROCAF F-16 has been greatly enhanced. The addition of a centre pedestal display to the cockpit provides a high-resolution display for sensor imagery, thereby improving tactical situational awareness and man-machine-interface. The original lightweight landing gear has also been replaced by a heavyweight version, enabling upgraded aircraft to carry heavier payloads.

While they may appear in the traditional colour scheme, upgraded aircraft have also been given a coat of Have Glass paint with radar cross-section reduction properties.

Initial Operational Capability (IOC) was supposed to be declared for the 4th TFW on 30 March 2021 but this was pushed back due to the crash of two F-5Es and loss of two pilots that same month.

Dassault Mirage 2000-5EI/DI[2]

Background

As the 1982 Communiqué had placed severe restrictions on arms sales to Taiwan, the island was keen to look elsewhere to modernise its military. In May 1989, then Chief of the General Staff Hau Pei-tsun visited France to propose the purchase of French arms, including the Mirage 2000. The 1989 Tiananmen Square Incident led to a souring of Sino-French relations and provided Taiwan an opportune moment to pursue the sale. For the French, the dissolution of the Soviet Union in 1991 had sparked concerns of a downward spiral of its arms industry, providing further impetus for the sale to move forward.

In response to French media reports that a deal of 120 Mirage 2000 fighters would be approved, the French government confirmed for the first time in May 1992 that it was evaluating such a sale. On 17 November that year, the French announced that a contract finalised at 60 aircraft – 48 single-seat 2000-5EI and 12 two-seat 2000-5DI – had been signed.

Inclusive of weapons and accessories, the deal – known to the Taiwanese as Project Fei Long (Flying Dragon) – was worth USD 3.8 billion. Despite the United States agreeing to sell the F-16, Taiwan viewed the purchase of the Mirage 2000 as an avenue to diversify its fighter fleet and avoid relying upon the US as its sole source.

ROCAF pilots first arrived at Mont-de-Marsan air base in 1994 for training on the aircraft. Among the initial cadre of instructor pilots was the late General Shen Yi-ming (then Lieutenant Colonel), who had been involved in F-16 test and evaluation work in the United States. Speaking to media during the inaugural Mirage 2000 delivery, he said that compared to the Americans, the French were more open to ROCAF pilots wearing their air force insignia on the base and were also more diligent in answering their queries.

Deliveries of all Mirage 2000s were made via ship as the securing of overflight and landing permits for ferry flights would have been impossible. The first batch of five aircraft arrived at the Port of Hualien on 5 May 1997. They were then towed to Hualien Air Base where inspection and assembly were conducted. The first of the aircraft arrived at its home base in Hsinchu 23 May and were received by the 499th TFW (today's 2th TFW).

Following the 1995-96 Taiwan Strait crisis, deliveries of the Mirage 2000s were sped up. All 60 aircraft were handed over by November 1998, brought forward by two years. Full Operational Capability (FOC) was subsequently declared on 10 May 2001.

Over the years, French and Taiwanese pilots have conducted frequent exchanges in each other units, providing an opportunity to build relationships and learn each other's capabilities and tactics. French pilots are typically assigned to the 2nd TFW's 48th Training Group during their tour in Taiwan. Since the loss of an exchange pilot in a French Mirage 2000 crash in 2012, the ROCAF has stopped sending personnel to France.

Five ROCAF Mirage 2000s have been lost over the years, resulting in the deaths of four crew members.

A 2th TFW Mirage-20005DI departs Hsinchu Air Base with a load of four MICA RF medium-range and two Magic II short-range air-to-air missiles. (Peter Ho)

Description

The aircraft's delta-wing configuration, coupled with the Snecma M53-P2 engine (21,400lb thrust), provides the Mirage 2000 an impressive climb rate of 985ft (300m) per second. This was a reason for the selection of the platform to assume the high-speed, high-altitude interceptor role from the F-104, which had similar performance characteristics. As mentioned in Chapter 2, the Mirage 2000s, like the F-104s previously, are based in Hsinchu to take advantage of the location's close proximity to the Chinese coast to allow the conduct of quick interceptions of intruding aircraft.

Due to political sensitivity, all ground modes of the Thales RDY radar have been removed, hence, relegating the Taiwanese Mirage 2000 to a purely air superiority fighter. Similarly, the aircraft's air-to-air refuelling capability has been eliminated. Like the Mirage 2000s of other users, ROCAF aircraft are fitted with the Integrated Countermeasure System (ICMS) from Thales.

Weapons and stores

As part of the deal, the ROCAF obtained 960 MICA RF medium-range and 480 Magic II short-range air-to-air missiles from Matra (today's MDBA). The MICA was the ROCAF's first active radar homing missile. When paired with the RDY radar, it provided the Mirage 2000 with a BVR capability that was then unmatched in the region.

As Taiwan was the first export customer for the MICA missile, there was considerable foreign interest in its capability. During what was the first firing of the missile outside France on 8 May 1998, a US Navy *Los Angeles*-class submarine was detected in the waters near the test range, most probably on a mission to gather telemetry data on the missile.

Delivered between 1996 and 1998, the solid rocket motors of the MICA and Magic 2 missiles were nearing the expiry of their shelf life by 2010. Members of the Legislative Yuan raised concerns about the reliability and safety of the solid rocket propellants in 2008, which was further amplified by the media. As a result of the focus, multiple batches of new rocket motors have since been ordered while a contract was separately awarded to NCSIST in 2016 to conduct a life extension of the missiles.

The ROCAF Mirage 2000s also employ the Thales ASTAC pod, an important component of the ROC military's electronic intelligence (ELINT) capabilities. Through the collection of electromagnetic emissions, the ASTAC system helps to build the PLA's electronic order of battle (EOB) for threat analysis. ROCAF Mirage 2000 on ELINT missions typically compose two aircraft: the ASTAC pod-carrying aircraft armed with a load of two Magic 2 missiles and an escort aircraft with a basic CAP load of two Magic 2 and two MICA missiles. A number of centreline DEFA 554 twin gun pods were also acquired for the two-seat Mirage 2000-5DIs as they lack an internal gun armament.

The 2th TFW Mirage-20005EI tail no. 2019 turns onto Hsinchu's runway 05 for an ELINT/combat air patrol mission. The aircraft is configured with an ASTAC port on its belly hardpoint and two Magic II air-to-air missiles. (Peter Ho)

The Mirage conundrum

The Mirage 2000's nearly 25 years of service has not been smooth. Early reports point to the aircraft facing corrosion issues due to Taiwan's humid weather and a higher concentration of pollutants in the Hsinchu area where they are based.

The ROCAF has also always been hard-pressed in maintaining the Mirage 2000 fleet to a high readiness standard. The support and life-cycle costs of the Mirage 2000 is the highest among the three second-generation fighters. Based on ROCAF budgetary figures in FY2020 the Mirage 2000's operations and maintenance cost per flight hour was about USD 28,500. This was significantly higher than the F-16A/B at USD 5,700 and USD 8,900 for the F-CK-1. With the diminishing availability of spare parts as the number of operational Mirage 2000s dwindle around the world, the support costs will continue to rise in the coming decade. As part of cost reduction measures, a number of Mirage 2000s have been placed under rotational storage in a humidity-controlled environment.

Between late 2009 and early 2010, the Mirage 2000s were also placed under the spotlight by the Taiwanese government and the media. Due to engine fan blade damage, availability of the aircraft fell below the mandated rate of 75 per cent while pilots were not receiving their stipulated 15 flying hours per month. The focus led to the diversion of substantial resources to purchase much needed spare parts and the devel-

A Mirage-2000SDI launches off the Changhua section of the No. 1 National Freeway during a highway drill as part of the Han Kuang 35 exercise in 2019. (Roy Choo)

opment of maintenance initiatives. Availability rates quickly recovered and pilots were clocking the required number of hours within months.

With the Mirage 2000 fleet more than halfway through the lifespan, there has been constant debates within the ROCAF on the future on the French fighter. While some have favoured a mid-life upgrade plan, it was understood that the ROCAF had made enquires with Dassault for such a program but have been provided with a proposal that was cost-prohibitive. The life-cycle costs and affordability issues are further compounded by the platform's lack of ability to undertake multi-role missions as well as its inability to integrate into the Hsun'an tri-service network, hence, further diminishing the cost-effectiveness of an upgrade.

It remains to be seen how much longer the Mirage 2000 will soldier on but a decision will soon have to be made as the supportability of the platform will sharply decline should it be maintained into the 2030s in its current configuration. The replacement of the Mirage 2000 by the F-16C/D Block 70s in the future is a possibility.

AIDC F-CK-1C/D Ching-kuo[3]

Background
In the late 1970s to early 1980s, Taiwan's attempts to procure its next generation fighter to replace aging Northrop F-5s and Lockheed F-104s have been met with failure. The United States, which was establishing relations with China, denied the Northrop F-20 Tigershark and the downgraded F-16/79. Negotiations to purchase the IAI Kfir were also unsuccessful. Hence, in line with a policy to develop self-reliance in defence technology, the ROC government decided to proceed with its Indigenous Defence Fighter (IDF) project in May 1982.

Before settling on the configuration, we are familiar with today, some of the proposals studied included a re-engineered F-104, as well as new designs that featured a cranked delta wing akin to the F-16XL and twin-tail delta wing designs, among others.

Led by the Aero Industry Development Centre (AIDC) – which had just been just newly integrated under NCSIST – the program was officially launched as Project An Hsiang (Safe Flight) in 1983. It was broken down into four development projects, each with its own focus area. Extensive guidance was provided by teams from American corporations embedded in each project. These comprise the:
- Ying Yang (Soaring Eagle) – airframe development in cooperation with General Dynamics
- Yun Han (Cloud Han) – engine development in cooperation with Garrett
- Tien Lei (Sky Thunder) – avionics development in cooperation with a variety of companies such as General Electric, Westinghouse etc
- Tien Chien (Sky Sword) – air-to-air missile development.

The first prototype of an eventual four was rolled out on 10 December 1988 and was named Ching Kuo in memory of the late President Chiang Ching-kuo. The maiden flight was accomplished six months later on 28 May 1989 to much fanfare. To evaluate the performance of the F-CK-1 (CK for Ching-kuo), 10 pre-production aircraft were delivered between 1992 and 1993.

While initial plans called for the production of 250 F-CK-1s, this was slashed to 130 when the US agreed to sell the F-16A/B in 1992. Deliveries of the F-CK-1A/Bs were first made to the 427th TFW (today's 3rd TFW) at CCK Air Base in 1992 to replace its F-104s. The wing was declared fully operational with the new type on 15 April 1997. This was followed by the 443rd TFW (today's 1st TFW) at Tainan Air Base, which began trading in its F-5E/Fs in 1997. It was commissioned as an F-CK-1 wing on 14 July 2000.

A pre-upgrade F-CK-1B in the markings of the 443rd TFW (today's 1st TFW)'s 3rd TFG arrives at Hsinchu Air Base during the Han Kuang 27 exercise in 2011. The aircraft is configured with a load of four AIM-9P Sidewinders and two TC-2 missiles, as well as a pair of 275-gallon drop tanks. (Peter Ho)

Mid-life upgrade

From 1998, post-production modifications were made to the F-CK-1 with the addition of improved radar warning receivers (RWR), combined interrogator/transponders and instrument landing systems. By 2001, the ROCAF was starting to look at a more comprehensive mid-life upgrade to improve the fighter's combat capabilities and address diminishing manufacturing sources and obsolescence issues. Taiwan MND began the allocation of USD 230 million for the project codenamed Hsiang Sheng.

The program included two phases:
- Avionics – upgrading of flight and mission computers, improvements to cockpit interface, replacement of radar components and identification friend or foe systems
- Weapons and fuel – incorporating enhanced weapon systems and conformal fuel tanks (CFTs)

With support from Lockheed Martin, AIDC produced two new prototypes of the F-CK-1 in the mid-life upgrade configuration. The prototype single-seater flew on 4 October 2006 and was followed by the twin-seater on 15 March 2007. In an unveiling ceremony one week later, the then President Chen Shui-bian named the newly configured aircraft the Hsiung Ying (Goshawk).

The prototypes would however be the only two aircraft that would receive this name. The ROCAF had misgivings about the upgrade, primarily centred on the problem of insufficient thrust that had bugged the F-CK-1, but now further compounded by the increased weight of the CFTs and structural modifications. Consequently, it was decided to proceed with the upgrade without the CFTs. Upgraded aircraft would thus be designated F-CK-1C/D but retain the Ching Kuo name.

The upgraded F-CK-1C/Ds feature enhanced man-machine interface with three coloured multi-function displays instead of the previous two. A BAE Systems 32-bit flight control computer was also adopted in replacement of a 16-bit system. Taking advantage of the improved computing power, source code for the flight controls were rewritten to improve the fighter's low-altitude autopilot capability. The F-CK-1's GD-53 Golden Dragon radar – which was based upon the AN/APG-67 – also had its sub-system modules reduced from five to three while new operating modes were introduced.

The retrofit of the aircraft to the new configuration was known as Project Hsiang Zhan, with work carried out in two phases. Between 2009 to 2013, the 71 Tainan-based F-CK-1s were upgraded at a cost of USD 598 million. The ROCAF was understood to be quite hesitant to proceed with the remaining 56 CCK-based aircraft since it was judged that the improvements afforded were marginal.

Tail no. 1502 taxies for departure from Hsinchu Air Base after supporting an aerial gunnery exercise. Since 2018, four F-CK-1Cs have been modified to carry the Meggitt RM-30B reeling machine-launcher and TDK-39 tow target. These are flown during AIDC-contracted target-towing, replacing F-5Es that were installed with the same system. (Peter Ho)

F-CK-1C tail no. 1458 returns to CCK Air Base after a captive-carry flight test of the TC-2C missile in June 2018. Developed under Project Ben Jian, the TC-2C provides enhanced performance over the TC-2 and can be rail-launched, thereby doubling maximum carriage. (Peter Ho)

Nonetheless, the ROCAF signed off on the USD 547 million upgrade project for the remaining aircraft. Work was conducted between 2014 to 2017, with the final two F-CK-1C/Ds handed over in December 2017. The 3rd FTW was declared fully operational on the upgraded aircraft on 9 March 2018.

The two F-CK-1C/D prototypes that had been placed in storage following their completion of test duties were also de-converted to Hsiang Zhan standard though the removal of CFTs and associated structural modifications. They were then inducted into the ROCAF as regular F-CK-1C/Ds in mid-2018, thereby taking the fleet size to 129.

Stretching over a decade, the F-CK-1 modernisation was considered a vital program by AIDC to help establish the upgrade and overhaul skillsets that would later come handy in the F-16V project.

Description

The F-CK-1 can be considered a lightweight fighter with relatively poor endurance and engine thrust. Due to political sensitivities, the United States was only willing to grant the Honeywell/ITEC TFE1042-70 (F125) afterburning turbofans, with two of these providing a combined thrust of 19,920lb. It is for this reason that the mission sets assigned to the F-CK-1 are generally at the lower levels of the airspace.

However, the ability of the F-CK-1 to scramble within five minutes of notice – compared to the six minutes of the F-16 and Mirage 2000 – is much cherished by the ROCAF.

The F-CK-1C/Ds are believed to still use the Litton (now Northrop Grumman) AN/ALR-85(V)1 RWRs that were introduced from the late 1990s.

F-CK-1D tail no. 1603 carries a Global Positioning System pod on its wingtip while performing a chase assignment in support of the XT-5 Yung Ying test program.
(Peter Ho)

Weapons and stores

The limited payload and range combination of the F-CK-1 has placed restrictions on certain aspects of its operational employment. Nevertheless, work-arounds have been attempted in order to provide the F-CK-1 with a decent level of weapons capability. Its armament is predominately indigenous, as detailed below:

Tien Chien 1 air-to-air missile

The Tien Chien 1 (TC-1) is a short-range infrared-guided missile analogous to the AIM-9L/M Sidewinder missile. Due to the sizable inventory of AIM-9P missiles left over after the decommissioning of many F-5E/Fs in the 1990s, production run for the TC-1 was limited to just 300 rounds. This has led to the common employment of the AIM-9P by both F-CK-1 wings while the TC-1 has been exclusively used by the 3rd TFW.

Tien Chien 2 air-to-air missile

Increased emphasis was placed by NCSIST on the development of the TC-2 as medium-range air-to-air missiles have been out of reach by the ROCAF. The TC-2 active radar homing missile – only one of a few at that time – is believed to incorporate the seeker design of the joint Motorola and Northrop's failed bid for the USAF/USN AMRAAM requirement. Few technical details of the TC-2 are available, but the missile is thought to have a range of 37 miles (60km). An F-CK-1 could carry only two of these missiles, both of which are mounted semi-recessed on the belly.

A longer-ranged version, the TC-2C, has been in development under Project Ben Jian. Believed to be able to engage targets up to 62 miles (100km) away, the missile also features a rail-launched ability. In contrast, the earlier variant could only be ejector-launched. This has enabled the doubling of the maximum carriage of the TC-2 to four, hence, strengthening the air-to-air capabilities of the F-CK-1.

Low-rate initial production of the TC-2C is expected to begin in 2021 while older missiles would be brought up to a similar standard. An anti-radiation version of the missile, known as the TC-2A, has had a protracted development stretching back to the early 2000s. There has been no updates nor sightings of the missile in recent years.

The United States government's consent to the sale of AGM-88 HARM missiles in 2017 might have sounded the death knell of this development.

Wan Chien cruise missile

As part of a drive to improve Taiwan's offensive posture, the F-CK-1C/Ds could be tasked to carry two Wan Chien standoff cruise missiles. Produced under Project Shen Fu (God's Axe) from 2015, each Wan Chien missile is equipped with a 771lb (350kg) sub-munitions load and could be targeted at enemy air and naval bases up to more than 125 miles (200km) away. An extended range version of the Wan Chien, capable of up to 250 miles (400km), is reported to be under development.

During a trip to Magong Air Base to visit the F-CK-1 Tian Ju detachment on 22 September 2020, President Tsai Ing-wen was shown an assortment of weapons, including a pair of Wan Chien missiles. The display was significant amidst rising cross-strait tensions as it signalled that the missiles were being stationed at the forward operating site close to the median line. Taiwan, like China, is not a signatory to the Convention on Cluster Munitions.

The F-CK-1 is also able to carry a range of general-purpose bombs including Mk 82, Mk 83 and CBU-100 cluster bombs. A weapon that the F-CK-1s has been long rumoured to employ is the indigenous Qing Yun (Green Cloud) fuel-air explosive.

Since 2018, four F-CK-1Cs modified to carry Meggitt RM-30B reeling machine-launcher and TDK-39 tow target, have been flown by contracted AIDC pilots to provide target towing services in support of ROCAF air gunnery exercises.

Weapon crews of the Tainan-based 1st TFW load a Wan Chien standoff cruise missile on a F-CK-1C as part of a readiness drill ahead of the Lunar New Year in January 2021. (Military News Agency)

Northrop F–5E/F Tiger II and RF–5E Tigergazor[4]

The ROCAF has been an ardent supporter of the F-5 family. It has operated the earliest F-5A/B Freedom Fighters attained through the United States Military Assistance Program; T-38A Talons in two separate leases; as well as the F-5E/F Tiger IIs. At its peak in the 1980s, over 300 F-5E/Fs had been in service with six ROCAF wings, all of these produced under licence by AIDC under Project Hu An (Peace Tiger). The introduction of its second-generation of fighters led to a gradual drawdown of the fleet.

At present, the F-5E/Fs are the most geriatric of the ROCAF fast jets. The youngest of these –F-5F tail no. 5416 – was rolled out in December 1986. Two dozen aircraft remain in service and have now been relegated to secondary duties. The majority of these are used by the 7th FTW in a lead-in fighter training (LIFT) role at Chihhang Air Base. F-5Es are also occasionally assigned the target-towing role for aerial gunnery training during the LIFT programme with the A/A37U-15 tow target.

Five RF-5E Tigergazor reconnaissance aircraft, converted by Singapore Technologies Aerospace in the late 1990s, remain in service alongside a handful of F-5F twin-seaters with the 12th TRG at Hualien Air base.

Structural and availability issues have plagued the ROCAF F-5E/F for years. AIDC had proposed an avionics and service life extension program known as the Tiger 2000 at the turn of the century, going as far as to build a prototype.

However, the ROCAF had showed little interest as it envisaged the replacement of the F-5 by a dedicated LIFT aircraft within a decade. Shifting timelines meant that the F-5 has soldiered on till today. The loss of an F-5E instructor pilot who did not survive ejection during a mishap on 29 October 2020 cast a spotlight on the state of the fleet.

F-5E and F-5F Tiger IIs of the Chihhang-based 7th FTW prepare to take off. The type has experienced poor availability and will be replaced by the T-5 Yung Ying in the 2020s. (Stephan de Brujin)

Converted by Singapore Technologies Aerospace in the late 1990s, five of the seven RF-5E Tigergazors remain in service with the Hualien-based 12th TRG.
(Stephan de Brujin)

There were calls to replace the ejection seats, which are nearly 40-years old. Just five months later, the fatal collision of two F-5Es on 22 March 2021 led to the ROCAF announcing it would upgrade the fleet with new Martin-Baker Mk 16 ejection seats from late 2021. The USD 27 million cost was seen as necessary as one of the F-5 pilots who ejected suffered similar brain hemorrhage injuries and likely hit his head against the canopy during ejection, similar to the previous incident. The replacement was also seen as insurance in case the phase-out of the F-5 could be delayed.

Current plans state that the AIDC T-5 Yung Ying (Brave Eagle) Advanced Jet Trainer will replace both the F-5 and AT-3 between 2021 and 2026. The delivery of MS-110 LOROP pods for F-16s in the later part of the decade would also ensure that the RF-5Es will be fully replaced.

Lockheed C-130H/HE Hercules[5]

The elderly Fairchild C-119 Flying Boxcar was in dire need for replacement by the early 1980s. The ROCAF had repeatedly sought the C-130 from the United States but was only offered the civilian L-100. The United States finally relented in June 1984 when it approved the sale of 12 C-130Hs. The first of these were delivered in December 1986 and began the replacement process of the C-119.

Two further batches of four C-130Hs each were purchased and delivered between the mid to late 1990s.

In additional, the ROCAF placed an order for a sole C-130H in 1990 for subsequent modification to an electronic warfare role. Delivery of the aircraft, tail no. 1351, was made to Pingtung in February 1993. Designated the C-130HE by the ROCAF, it features distinctive fairings under the nose, atop the tail and on the belly. It is apparently known within the air force as the Tian Gan (Sky Interference) aircraft. Speculations of the aircraft's roles centre around both signals intelligence (SIGINT) and the electronic jamming of radars. Otherwise, little else is known about the aircraft.

One C-130H has been lost in an accident in 1997 while attempting to perform a go-around at Songshan airport under inclement weather. The remaining 19 C-130s are flown by the 101st and 102nd Airlift Squadrons from Pingtung South. The C-130HE is operated by the 6th Electronic Warfare Squadron at the same base.

Apart from cargo transport and re-supply missions, the ROCAF C-130s are also used in cloud-seeding operations during the dry season when water levels in reservoirs could fall below stipulated limits.

The C-130s can also be easily converted for VIP transportation through the use of roll-on/roll-off cabin pallets.

The C-130s are considered the most well-travelled aircraft in the ROCAF fleet. Over the last two decades, it has been deployed on humanitarian aid delivery missions. On several of such occasions, some countries have requested that the ROCAF black out its insignia on the aircraft to avoid any political fallout.

It is also worth noting that few modifications have been made to the C-130s since their delivery 20 years ago. Their survivability in combat operations is questionable due to their lack of RWRs, missile alert warning (MAW) systems and decoy launchers. The ROCAF has announced its intention to put the fleet through an avionics upgrade and is considering contender proposals.

Understood to be known within the ROCAF as the Tian Gan, C-130HE tail no. 1351 is believed to perform SIGINT and electronic jamming roles. (Eric Lai)

Northrop Grumman E-2K Hawkeye

Concerns about political sensitivity initially saw the United States agreeing to provide only refurbished ex-USN E-2Bs for Taiwan's airborne early warning requirement. These would have been fitted with the APS-138 radar used on E-2C Group 0 aircraft. It subsequently agreed to sell new-built E-2C Group 2 aircraft fitted with the APS-145 system on condition that the sale was recorded as E-2Bs. For this purpose, a number of parts would be symbolically taken from E-2Bs so that the new aircraft would feature their USN Bureau Numbers (BuNo). A request was also made for a tactical data link, but this was denied as it was considered to have surpassed its legitimate defence requirements. Eventually, in August 1993, four E-2T Hawkeyes were ordered in a USD 749.5 million deal.

In May 1995, the first E-2T rolled off the Northrop Grumman's St. Augustine facility. All four aircraft were transported by sea in pairs of two, arriving in Taiwan in September 1995. They were commissioned into service with the 2nd Early Warning Squadron at Pingtung North Air Base in November that year, heralding a new era in ROCAF air surveillance and detection capabilities.

The fleet of four aircraft was deemed insufficient for its operational capability and plans were made for a further two aircraft. A USD 400 million deal for a further two E-2s, this time of the E-2T Hawkeye 2000 standard, were approved in July 1999. Delivered in August and November 2004, they were similarly shipped to Taiwan, arriving in May 2005. The newer aircraft were designated the E-2K, an abbreviation of the USN nomenclature for the E-2C Hawkeye 2000 – HE2K. Compared to the older E-2Ts, the air-

Nineteen C-130H transport aircraft are operated by the 101st and 102nd Airlift Squadrons at Pingtung South Air Base.
(Stephan de Brujin)

craft are fitted with two NP2000 eight-bladed propellers, a mission computer upgrade (MCU), advanced control indicator set (ACIS), updated identification friend or foe systems and software updates. ROCAF aircraft are not equipped with the cooperative engagement capabilities (CEC) and Satellite Communications (SATCOM) capability.

With the delivery of the newer aircraft, plans were made to bring the previous four, which had then been in service for 15 years, to the latest standard. As part of a larger arms deal to Taiwan, a USD 250 million FMS notification for the upgrade was announced in October 2008. The E-2Ts were shipped back to the United States in pairs for the upgrade one year apart in 2010 and 2011. Post-upgrade, the first pair returned in December 2011 followed by the second pair in March 2013, finally bringing the ROCAF airborne early warning and control (AEW&C) capability to full strength.

The ROCAF's six Northrop Grumman E-2K Hawkeyes are among the most important assets in the ROC military. Tasked with the airborne detection of adversary aircraft and missiles, they not only help in filling gaps in radar coverage but also provide a critical back-up to ground-based radar stations should they be rendered inoperative. A lesser-known role of the Hawkeye is that of communications relay. The capability was put to good use during humanitarian assistance and disaster relief effort during the Jiji earthquake in 1999 and Typhoon Morakot in 2009. Orbiting over the Central Mountain Range on round-the-clock duties, the E-2s managed the constant flow of disaster relief helicopters flying through the valleys between east and west Taiwan. According to local media reports in early 2020, Taiwan will spend USD 51.4 million to study a further upgrade of the six E-2Ks.

E-2K tail no. 2501 is one of four E-2Ts purchased in 1993 and was upgraded to E-2K standard in the early 2010s. Today, all six E-2K Hawkeyes perform an important AEW&C role and provide a back-up to ground-based radars should they be knocked out in times of war. (Stephan de Brujin)

Lockheed P-3C Orion[6]

In its later years, Taiwan's antiquated S-2T Trackers suffered from poor mission availability and were unable to track the latest Chinese submarines. The program to purchase 12 P-3Cs as a replacement began under the ROC Navy as Project Shen Ou. Twelve brand-new P-3Cs were first approved by the United States government in a 2001 arms sales package. However, the USD 4.1 billion price tag, which factored in the re-opening of Lockheed Martin's production line, created much political controversy and was deemed too expensive. Taiwan began looking at alternative solutions such as surplus USN aircraft.

Six years later, a contract worth USD 1.9 billion for 12 refurbished P-3Cs was placed in 2007.

Twelve 1970s-vintage former USN P-3Cs were drawn from storage at the Aerospace Maintenance and Regeneration Group in Tucson, Arizona and received new wings and a structural service life extension program, as well as an avionics upgrade, bringing them to the latest P-3C standard. They were also given the capability to launch the AGM-65 Maverick and AGM-84 Harpoon for anti-surface warfare as well as Mk 46 and Mk 54 torpedoes for sub-surface work.

The P-3C program was later transferred to the ROCAF when the anti-submarine warfare mission was handed over in July 2013. The first P-3C was delivered in September 2013, and the final arrived in June 2017. All 12 aircraft are in service with the 33rd and 34th Squadrons at Pingtung North Air Base.

Increased Chinese navy activity in recent years have kept the P-3Cs busy monitoring these movements. The PLA incursions into the southwestern corner of Taiwan's ADIZ have also seen the use of P-3Cs as intercepting aircraft in late 2020.

The offensive punch of the ROCAF P-3C Orions comes in the form of AGM-65 Maverick and AGM-84 Harpoon missiles for anti-surface warfare and Mk 46 and Mk 54 torpedoes for anti-submarine warfare.
(Peter Ho)

The Special Transport Squadron at Songshan Air Base is assigned 12 Beech 1900Cs. Apart from administrative transport, one aircraft is loaned to the Flight Training Command for airlift training.
(Peter Ho)

This sole Boeing 737-800, tail no. 3701 is operated by the Presidential Flight Squadron to provide executive transport for the leader.
(Peter Ho)

Three Fokker 50 aircraft in service with the Special Transport Squadron are used as administrative transport for the country's leadership and military officials.
(Peter Ho)

Beech 1900C

An order for 12 Beech 1900Cs was placed in October 1987 to fulfil the role of administrative transport, replacing C-47 Skytrains that were previously used in this assignment. Delivered from 1988, two of these aircraft – tail numbers 1911 and 1912 – are known as EBH-1900s and are used for the tests and calibration of navigation aids. They can be distinguished from the rest of the fleet with their orange and white paint scheme. One aircraft is loaned to the Flight Training Command at Gangshan for airlift training.

Boeing 737-800

A Boeing 737-800 has been operated by the Presidential Flight Squadron since February 2000. The aircraft replaced a Boeing 737-400 which had been leased from China Airlines as a stop-gap solution when the last of four elderly Boeing 727-100s were phased out in 1998.

Including incumbent President Tsai Ing-wen, four past presidents have flown on the aircraft. In recent times, the aircraft has been mostly used for domestic transport missions, with the preference for a leased commercial airliner for international trips. Over the 20 years of service, the aircraft has been used mostly for visits to the Pacific island nations, which are among the last countries with diplomatic ties to Taiwan.

Fokker 50

The ROCAF took delivery of three Fokker 50 administrative transport aircraft in 1992. Two of these are configured in a 28-seat executive cabin layout while the other is in a 38-seat layout. The Fokker 50s are flown by the Special Transport Squadron for the movement of the country's leadership and military officials.

Tail no. 1912 is one of two EBH-1900s utilised for the testing and calibration of navigation aids. Both aircraft are painted in a high-visibility scheme.
(Peter Ho)

AIDC AT-3 Tzu Chiang

The AT-3 was developed by AIDC as a replacement for the Air Force Academy's T-33 advanced trainers. The first of two prototypes conducted its maiden flight in September 1980, leading to the production of more than 60 aircraft between 1984 to 1989. The type was named the Tzu Chiang (Resilience).

AIDC developed two prototypes of a single-seat version – the XA-3 – and modified an AT-3 for a combat capable aircraft requirement. The aircraft were also modified with the HF-2 anti-ship missile for a possible anti-ship aircraft requirement for the ROC Navy. Interest in the respective requirements waned and the project did not progress beyond the prototype stage.

The AT-3 is also flown by the ROCAF's aerobatic display team, the Thunder Tiger.

Beechcraft T-34 Mentor

About 30 of the 44 T-34s purchased by the ROCAF in 1985 remain in service. Prospective pilots take their first step in flight training on the aircraft at the ROCAF Academy's Flight Training Command. Talk of replacement of the T-34 has been going on for years, with the Beechcraft T-6 Texan II spoken of as a replacement at one stage in 2015.

While predominately used as an advanced trainer at the Flight Training Command, AT-3s could take on a combat assignment if required. The CD-1 jamming pod was developed by NCSIST to provide the AT-3 with an electronic warfare role. AT-3 tail no. 0862 carries a pair of the pods during a Han Kuang exercise at Chiayi Air Base in 2013.
(Peter Ho)

Air Rescue Group[7]

The control and coordination of Taiwan's national search and rescue (SAR) service rests with the National Rescue Command Centre. In the event that a helicopter SAR operation is required, it could call upon the National Airborne Service Corps (NASC) – an agency under the Ministry of the Interior – or the ROCAF's Air Rescue Group (ARG). The majority of civilian SAR operations are conducted by the NASC but the ARG could step in when called upon.

Based at Chiayi Air Base with detachments in Chihhang and Songshan, the ARG, or more commonly referred to as the Seagull Rescue Team, currently operates a helicopter fleet comprising three Airbus Helicopters EC225 Super Puma, three Sikorsky S-70C-6 Super Bluehawks and 14 UH-60M Black Hawks.

Fifteen UH-60Ms were transferred from the ROC Army to replace 13 elderly S-70C-1/1As from December 2018. One of these was lost in a high-profile crash in January 2020 during a VIP transport mission. Seven personnel on board, including two crew members and Chief of the General Staff Shen Yi-ming died in the crash. There are plans for five UH-60Ms to be modified for all weather and night operations.

The three EC225s and three S-70C-6s are fully capable all-weather SAR helicopters. For mountain rescue missions, the preference would be to deploy the S-70C-6s and UH-60Ms over the EC225 due to their superior performance in hot and high-altitude conditions.

The ROC military's combat SAR (CSAR) capability is at its infancy. Training for such a mission only started in recent years, presumably with the UH-60Ms of the ARG or those of the ROC Army Aviation and Special Forces Command.

Around 30 T-34s remain in service today with the Flight Training Command at Gangshan Air Base. After being used in the basic training role for only around five years, it was realised the AIDC T-CH-1 – a copy of the T-28 Trojan – was too powerful for the assignment. In the early 1980s, 44 T-34Cs were acquired to replace them.
(Peter Ho)

Three EC225s were purchased for SAR operations in 2009 and were commissioned into service with the ARG in July 2012. (Peter Ho)

Four Sikorsky S-70C-6 Super Bluehawks were introduced in 1998, boosting the ARG's all-weather SAR capability. One was lost with five crew members during a rescue mission at sea near Lanyu island in March 2012. (Peter Ho)

Beginning in December 2018, 15 UH-60M Black Hawks were transferred from the ROC Army to the ARG. Fourteen remain in service. (Peter Ho)

ROCAF FUTURE PROGRAMS AND PROSPECTS

Roy Choo

The final chapter provides an update on the ROCAF future aircraft programs and contemplates what the future holds for the air arm.

Lockheed Martin F-16C/D Block 70 Fighting Falcon[1]

Although the ROCAF received 340 of what it calls the second-generation fighters in the 1990s, this was still short of its estimated requirement of 450 aircraft.

In 2006, Taiwan officially made known its intention to purchase 66 F-16C/Ds at the Monterey Talks – a series of US-Taiwan bilateral meetings on national security. Multiple Letters of Requests have been sent over the years for such a purchase, but the United States government has consistently refused to consider. A United States DoD presentation to Congress in September 2011 argued that F-16C/Ds did not meet Taiwan's needs as they were too dependent on runways that would be vulnerable to PLA SRBMs. Ironically, an upgrade package of ROCAF F-16A/Bs was passed that month – widely seen as a consolation price. Lobby groups continued fighting for the sale, arguing that the F-16A/B mid-life upgrade would result in a fighter gap as aircraft are taken out of service and cycled into the retrofit line.

The United States government finally relented under the Trump administration in 2019, when a notification for 66 F-16C/D Block 70s was announced on 20 August 2019. The package, worth an estimated USD 8 billion, also included APG-83 AESA radars, ALE-50 towed decoys, APX-126 advanced identification friend or foe, plus other miscellaneous equipment and technical support.

The delivery schedule for the program, internally named Feng Xiang (Phoenix Soaring) calls for the first F-16C and F-16D to be delivered by 2023 for initial testing, while the last are expected to be delivered by 2026. According to official documents, 56 of the aircraft will be single-seaters, with the remaining 10 twin-seaters

While sharing many common features with the upgraded F-16Vs, the new-built F-16C/Ds will be powered by General Electric F110-GE-129 engines, which present a slight increase in thrust, but more importantly, serve to avoid a potential fleet-wide grounding due to engine technical issues. The Block 70 will also be equipped with conformal fuel tanks for extended-range operation – a significant requirement considering the ROCAF does not operate aerial refuelling tankers.

A Chiayi-based 4th TFW F-16V returns from a combat air patrol with a load of two AIM-9M Sidewinder and four AIM-120C AMRAAM air-to-air missiles during heightened tensions in the Taiwan Strait in June 2020. (Peter Ho)

At the Taipei Aerospace & Defence Technology Exhibition in August 2019, an F-16 model commissioned by Lockheed Martin created somewhat of a stir as it was displayed with an unidentified pod on its port intake hard point, likely to be an infrared search and track sensor. If delivered, this will greatly enhance the ROCAF's capability to passively detect Chinese fighters, particularly the low-observable J-20.

In 2020, the ROCAF was also believed to have signed contract for the L3Harris ALQ-254 Viper Shield embedded electronic warfare suite for the F-16C/Ds.

Plans for induction have not been announced, but it has been made known that they will be based at Chihhang Air Base where re-development work costing USD 116 million is planned to bed down the new fighters. Meanwhile, lead-in fighter training (LIFT) will move to Gangshan. If followed through, 7th FTW will be re-named the 7th TFW and would operate the new fighters.

AIDC T-5 Yung Ying[2]

Replacement of the obsolete F-5E/F in the LIFT role has proved to be an enduring problem the ROCAF. In the late 2000s and early 2010s, the ROCAF examined an option to convert a wing of F-CK-1s to perform the training role and retire the F-5s. This was on the condition that it could purchase a wing of new fighters, which had not been attainable till 2019.

The ROCAF also explored the purchase of new jet trainers. It evaluated the KAI T-50 Golden Eagle and the Leonardo M-346. In 2014, a Memorandum of Understanding (MOU) was signed between AIDC and Leonardo (then Alenia Aermacchi) for the co-build of the M-346 fitted with substantial indigenous content. At about the same time,

AIDC also promoted a modernised AT-3 called the AT-3 MAX – fitted with updated glass cockpit and avionics – and a jet trainer version of the F-CK-1 twin-seater, then dubbed the XT-5.

When President Tsai Ing-wen took office in 2016, she made indigenous defence production a central pillar of the island's defence policy, consequently putting the M-346 out of favour. A tender was called for and the T-5 was officially selected. A USD 2.2 billion deal was signed with NCSIST on 7 February 2017 for 66 aircraft, ground-based training systems (GBTS), mission planning systems, basic flight simulators and training support equipment. NCSIST, in turn, sub-contracted AIDC to develop the aircraft. The T-5 will replace the AT-3s and F-5s currently operated in the advanced training and LIFT roles respectively. The pilot training system will thus be streamlined from three aircraft types to two.

The first XT-5 prototype was unveiled by President Tsai on 24 September 2019 at AIDC's Shalu complex. The aircraft, one of two flight test prototypes and two static test prototypes, was named Yung Ying (Brave Eagle). Although based upon the design of the twin-seat version of the F-CK-1, over 80 per cent new components were incorporated. Among changes are the increased use of composite materials for weight reduction, greater fuel capacity, a thicker wind chord for slower, more stable low-level flight, removal of the gun and radar, and the use of the non-afterburning Honeywell/ITEC F124-200TW.

A locally developed ZAH-1400A network communication radio will function as a datalink to the GBTS and will allow the receiving of flight scenarios, threats and friendlies in what would be a live-virtual construct training environment. To circumvent the lack of a stepped tandem cockpit, a 4K full-colour liquid crystal display will be fitted at the rear cockpit to provide a high-definition view of the front.

The first XT-5 Yung Ying prototype tail no. 11001 was unveiled in September 2019 and conducted its maiden flight in June 2020.
(Peter Ho)

The first prototype of the T-5 conducted its maiden flight on 22 June 2020, followed by a second on 25 December 2020. The developmental test phase was completed in February 2021 and operational test began the following month. The schedule as of November 2020 calls for the delivery of the first two aircraft by 2021, with the remaining 64 between 2022 to 2026. Initial aircraft go towards the replacement of the F-5, followed by the AT-3s. This will see the LIFT program moved from Chihhang and incorporated into the Air Force Academy's Flight Training Command in Gangshan.

Many have been sceptical of the T-5 and wonder if the training gap between the platform and the T-34 would be too huge. Others have wondered if it would have been more cost-effective to purchase an existing model. Time will tell if this decision will be the right one.

Unmanned aerial vehicle programs[3]

Compared with the mainland, Taiwan lags far behind in both the operation and development of unmanned aerial vehicles (UAVs). As of 2020, the only two UAVs in active service are the Rui Yuan (Albatross) in service with ROC Navy and the Hung Chueh (Cardinal) hand-launched system used by ROC Army Special Forces and ROC Marine Corps, both developed by NCSIST.

The Teng Yun (Cloud Rider) medium-altitude long-endurance (MALE) UAV system has been in development by NCSIST's Aeronautical System Research Division (ASRD) since 2009. Three early development models were produced in the early 2010s. This was followed by two prototypes of a first version (tail nos. 1611 and 1612), with a mock-up showcased at TADTE 2015. In response to ROCAF feedback, a second version (prototype tail nos. 1811 and 1812) was developed. Bearing a resemblance to the General Atomics MQ-9 Reaper, it incorporates a new airframe design, larger wings and a more prominent engine inlet. Honeywell TPE331 turboprop engines were also purchased to address insufficient engine thrust issues of the Rotax 914F used in the previous model. Extensive testing of the Teng Yun began at Chihhang Air Base in late

Teng Yun tail no. 1612 on display at the 2017 Hualien Air Base Open Day. This is one of two prototypes of the earlier version of the Teng Yun that was produced in the mid-2010s. (Peter Ho)

2020. A Teng Yun prototype – which appears to be that of the first version – encountered issues while approaching Chihhang for landing on 18 February 2021 and crashed in forested area near the air base. Production of the Teng Yun is expected to begin in 2024. The UAV would likely be armed with air-to-ground munitions and could also be used in an electronic warfare role.

Another local system that is under development and is being acquired by the ROCAF's Air Defence and Artillery Command is the Chien Hsiang truck-launched anti-radiation drone.

To augment its indigenous capabilities in light of the protracted development of the Teng Yun, Taiwan will also acquire four 'weapons-ready' MQ-9Bs. The approval of the USD 600 million FMS was announced on 3 November 2020 and included SeaVue maritime patrol radars and SAGE 750 electronic support measures (ESM) systems, which would essentially make them the SeaGuardian variant. Taiwan has expressed interest in the MQ-9's predecessor – the RQ-1 Predator – as early as the mid-2000s but a purchase has not been permitted due to the ban of export of Category 1 unmanned aircraft systems under the Missile Technology Control Regime (MTCR). The MQ-9B deal came within four months after the Trump administration reinterpreted the policy.

UAVs are expected to play an important role under its asymmetric-focussed ODC defence strategy. Through a hi-lo mix, a small number of matured and highly capable MQ-9Bs could be used alongside a larger fleet of Teng Yun systems to fulfil ISR and strike missions.

Future fighter programs[4]

While the 66 new F-16C/Ds will address the ROCAF's fighter capability shortfall to some extent, new aircraft will be required from the 2030s as upgraded F-16Vs and F-CK-1C/Ds reach the end of their lifespan.

The ROCAF has eyed the F-35 for some time now, specifically the F-35 short-take off and vertical landing (STOVL) variant. According to a Shephard Media article, Taiwan had submitted a letter of intent and requests for price and availability data as far back as 2002 for between 100 to 150 F-35A/Bs. It added that its ability to generate airpower will be severely curtailed after initial strikes against its airbases, hence, an aircraft with STOVL capability will be required. Repeated requests were also made for three squadrons of F-35Bs during the Trump administration.

The F-35Bs' low observable characteristics and its ability to use short unprepared strips will be a quantum leap for Taiwan's airpower capabilities. However, it is apparent that the United States will not approve any F-35 sale to Taiwan at this stage as it would have gone too far across 'the red line', with regard to weapon sales to the island. American concerns about potential leaks of such a sensitive weapon and Taiwan's ability to afford the purchase of a useful quantity make any sale of the F-35 unlikely in the near future.

There has also been chatter from government sources, including from then defence minister Feng Shih-kuan in 2017, about the indigenous development of a new generation of fighters. No details or design was spoken of then but any such project will be entirely dependent on the support of the United States. In April 2021, the NCSIST revealed that research is ongoing in the design and development of such a fighter and its engine.

Outstanding needs[5]

The ROCAF has a significant number of outstanding capability requirements yet to be fulfilled. Budget constraints meant many of such needs have been postponed indefinitely and forgotten. Some of these include a basic trainer to replace the T-34, and a light-medium tactical transport in the class of the Leonardo C-27J or Airbus C295.

One capability that the ROCAF truly requires is an aerial refuelling aircraft that would provide a force-multiplier effect for its fighter force. During peacetime, an air-refuelling capability could keep fighters on CAPs aloft for longer durations to maintain a deterrent presence. This is particularly required at the corners of its ADIZ that are far from the main island where the PLA has regularly projected its presence into. In combat operations, a tanker aircraft would also be handy to keep fighters airborne while airfield repair teams bring an inoperative runway back to working order.

Taiwan was understood to have been offered ex-USAF KC-135s through the Pentagon's Excess Defense Articles (EDA) program in the late 1990s but the leadership at that time saw no requirement for such a capability. Taiwan has made requests to purchase surplus KC-135s as recently as 2018 but has not made any headway. It is also noteworthy that the efficacy of old and maintenance-intensive KC-135s is uncertain. Boeing KC-46A and Airbus A330 Multi-Role Tanker Transport aircraft – the latter either newly built or converted from pre-owned airliners – could present an option. Even if attainable, it is not known if the defence budget could accommodate such a purchase in the near-term.

Taiwan's airborne electronic warfare capabilities are also relatively weak and appear to be dependent on the C-130HE, as far as available information suggests. New and enhanced platforms that could effectively exploit or deny the use of the electromagnetic spectrum could help blunt the edge of the PLA. For example, through SIGINT and ELINT, hidden PLA SRBM TELs could be geo-located and identified for subsequent destruction once they receive launch orders from higher headquarters. Taiwan was known to have requested price and availability data for SIGINT aircraft in 2002.

Conclusion

When this book was written in 2020–21, the ROCAF was under pressure from the PLA's unrelenting grey-zone assault and it does not look like it will get any easier. Sustained efforts must be made by the ROCAF leadership to challenge existing concepts of operations and think how the playbook can be improved to suit the new circumstances.

Some commentators have mentioned that Taiwan's greatest enemy is not on the outside, but from within. Taiwan's less than ideal civil-military relationship and partisan infighting have done more damage to the ROC military, while it struggles to modernise amid the renewed threat. It is perhaps poignant that the island stakeholders evaluate what really is at stake should the ROCAF, and the armed forces as a whole, fail to safeguard the defence of the island.

APPENDIX I:
PATCHES OF ROCAF AIR UNITS

ROCAF Command HQ

Combatant Command

Education, Training and Doctrine Development Command

Maintenance and Logistics Command

Air Defence and Artillery Command

Tainan Air Base

1st TFW

1st TFG
'Gymnogyps'
F–CK–1C/D

3rd TFG
'Celestial Eagle'
F–CK–1C/D

9th TFG
'Bugs Bunny'
F–CK–1C/D

Hsinchu Air Base

2nd TFW

41st TFG

M2000–DI/EI

42nd TFG
'Cobra'
M2000–DI/EI

48th TG

M2000–DI/EI

Ching Chuan Kang Air Base

3rd TFW

7th TFG
'Coyote'
F–CK–1C/D

28th TFG
'Baby Dragon'
F–CK–1C/D

ATRDC

OTEG

As required

AIDC

86

Chiayi Air Base

4th TFW

21st TFG
'Gamblers'
F–16A/B/V
Block 20

22nd TFG
'Condor'
F–16A/B/V
Block 20

23rd TFG
'Tzu Chiang'
F–16A/B/V
Block 20

ARG
'Seagull'
EC225, S–70C–6,
UH–60M

Hualien Air Base

5th TCW

12th TRG
'Tigergazer'
RF–5E, F–5F,
F–16 Block 20

17th TFG
'Thunder'
F–16A/B
Block 20

26th TFG
'Witch'
F–16A/B
Block 20

27th TFG
'Black Dragon'
F–16A/B
Block 20

Pingtung North Air Base

6th CW

ASW Group

33rd Sqn

P–3C

34th Sqn
'Black Bat'
P–3C

20th EWG

2nd EW Sqn

E–2K

Pingtung South Air Base

6th CW

10th TAG
'Camel'

101st AS
'Cattle'
C-130H

102nd AS
'Horse'
C-130H

20th EWG

6th EW Sqn

C-130HE

Chihhang Air Base

7th FTW

7th FTG

44h FTS

F-5E/F

45th FTS
'Black Panther'
F-5E/F

46th FTS
'Aggressors'
F-5E/F

Gangshan Air Base

**Air Force
Academy**

FTC

BTS

T-34C-1

FTS

AT-3

ATS

BH-1900

ITS

T-34C-1, AT-3

Aerobatic Team
'Thunder Tiger'

AT-3

Songshan Air Base

Songshan AB Command

Special Transport Sqn

BH-1900, Fokker 50

Presidential Flight Sqn

737-800

Luke AFB, Arizona, US

56th FW
'Thunderbolts'

21st FS
'Gamblers'

F-16A/B

Edwards AFB, California, US

412th TW

416th FTS

F-16V

BIBLIOGRAPHY

Endnotes CHAPTER 1

Black Bat squadron1

1   Pocock, C., *The Black Bats: CIA Spy Flights over China from Taiwan* (Centreville: Schiffer Publishing, 2010) ISBN 978-0764335136 https://air.mnd.gov.tw/EN/Unit/Activity_Detail.aspx?CID=173&ID=113

Assistance to Singapore's fledging air force

2   https://wikileaks.org/plusd/cables/1976SINGAP04704_b.html https://xinguozhi.wordpress.com/2017/01/30/%E6%98%9F%E5%85%89%E8%AE%A1%E5%88%92%E5%8F%8A%E5%8F%B0%E6%98%9F%E5%86%9B%E4%BA%8B%E4%BA%A4%E6%B5%81/ Lee, K.Y., *From Third World to First: The Singapore Story: 1965-2000* (Times Edition, 2000) ISBN 978-9812049841 https://eresources.nlb.gov.sg/printheritage/image.aspx?id=a5694220-6934-4b9d-a296-8c00d49d66fc

3   http://www.taipeitimes.com/News/taiwan/archives/2019/01/29/2003708858

Endnotes CHAPTER 2

1   https://www.youtube.com/watch?v=qsA9cGRhD8c

2   https://www.youtube.com/watch?v=PYacED3RcMU&feature=youtu.be https://www.the-northrop-f-5-enthusiast-page.info/

3   https://user.guancha.cn/main/content?id=185133 http://www.taipeitimes.com/News/taiwan/archives/2012/10/01/2003544098 https://project2049.net/wp-content/uploads/2018/05/revolutionizing_taiwans_security_leveraging_c4isr_for_traditional_and_non_traditional_challenges.pdf Ding, A. S., 'Taiwan: From Integrated Missile Defence to RMA' *The Information Revolution in Military Affairs in Asia*, pp. 167-184 (London: Palgrave MacMillan, 2004) ISBN 978-1403964670

4   https://news.tvbs.com.tw/politics/1038688

5   https://www.upmedia.mg/news_info.php?SerialNo=98931

6   http://minnickarticles.blogspot.com/2010/05/taiwans-hidden-base-will-safeguard.html

https://project2049.net/2017/11/08/risk-and-resiliency-chinas-emerging-air-base-strike-threat/https://www.upmedia.mg/news_info.php?SerialNo=98931

7   https://udn.com/news/story/10930/4981352?fbclid=IwAR11K5HVLieWzSzf_twsfYr2pQfFEtBsy8d3YUDDyKRcPlduJcNb66sCpEU https://www.taiwannews.com.tw/en/news/3998010

8   http://www.taipeitimes.com/News/taiwan/archives/2011/09/14/2003513241

Endnotes CHAPTER 3

1   https://www.forbes.com/sites/lorenthompson/2020/09/29/why-taiwan-has-become-the-geographical-pivot-of-history-in-the-pacific-age/?sh=43c9ca751921

2   https://warontherocks.com/2017/02/has-china-been-practicing-preemptive-missile-strikes-against-u-s-bases/ https://project2049.net/2017/11/08/risk-and-resiliency-chinas-emerging-air-base-strike-threat/

3   https://www.channelnewsasia.com/news/commentary/china-jet-fighter-plane-america-more-powerful-military-air-force-13776138 https://media.defense.gov/2020/Sep/01/2002488689/-1/-1/1/2020-DOD-CHINA-MILITARY-POWER-REPORT-FINAL.PDF

4   https://www.us-taiwan.org/wp-content/uploads/2019/12/2010_may11_balance_of_air_power_taiwan_strait.pdf

5   https://www.taipeitimes.com/News/editorials/archives/2005/05/25/2003256559 https://sentinel.tw/taiwans-air-to-air-missile-shortage-a-critical-vulnerability/ Easton, I., *The Chinese Invasion Threat: Taiwan's Defence and American Strategy in Asia* (Manchester: Eastbridge Books, 2019) ISBN 978-1-788691765

6   https://jamestown.org/program/military-activity-and-political-signaling-in-the-taiwan-strait-in-early-2020/ https://cn.reuters.com/article/idINIndia-58447620110726 https://www.taipeitimes.com/News/taiwan/archives/2020/10/23/2003745648

7   CHEN, Y., 'The Shifting Balance of Air Superiority at the Taiwan
    Strait and its Implications on Taiwan's Defence Planning.' *Taiwan's
    Security and Air Power*, pp. 37–51 (London: Routledge, 2004)
    ISBN 978-1138371200
    https://jamestown.org/program/the-evolution-of-taiwans-military-
    strategy-convergence-and-dissonance/?fbclid=IwAR0XP7TMkA4TL
    W7Q_mbU-4lDe9efkaOmH8-DCmz_M0WEJ6fzTnl2o5_mbOo
    MURRAY, W. S., 'Revisiting Taiwan's Defense Strategy', *Naval War
    College Review*, Vol. 61, No. 3, Article 3, 2008
    https://www.rand.org/pubs/research_reports/RR1051.html
    https://thediplomat.com/2020/11/taiwans-overall-defense-concept-
    explained/
    https://www.ustaiwandefense.com/tdnswp/wp-content/
    uploads/2020/02/Taiwan-National-Defense-Report-2019.pdf
    https://www.aei.org/articles/taiwans-high-end-and-low-end-defense-
    capabilities-balance/

8   TAYLOR, B., *Dangerous Decade: Taiwan's Security and Crisis Man-
    agement* (London: Routledge, 2019) ISBN 978-0367437480
    https://project2049.net/2020/09/01/preparing-for-the-nightmare-
    readiness-and-ad-hoc-coalition-operations-in-the-taiwan-strait/
    https://www.taipeitimes.com/News/editorials/
    archives/2010/02/22/2003466301
    https://www.bbc.com/news/world-asia-pacific-12401472

9   https://www.cna.com.tw/news/aipl/202008280061.aspx

Endnotes CHAPTER 4

1   https://theme.udn.com/theme/story/6773/2404128
    https://focustaiwan.tw/politics/202012030023
    https://www.us-taiwan.org/wp-content/uploads/2019/12/2012_the_
    looming_taiwan_fighter_gap.pdf
    https://focustaiwan.tw/politics/202012060014

2   https://www.youtube.com/watch?v=lDXEUe96f9g
    http://www.taipeitimes.com/News/taiwan/
    archives/2017/10/27/2003681137
    https://www.taipeitimes.com/News/taiwan/
    archives/2010/03/22/2003468632
    http://www.taiwanairpower.org/af/mirage.html
    https://tw.appledaily.com/politics/20190916/PUS4GR7EELB4JJ-
    COUBZ6EBEHHA/
    https://www.us-taiwan.org/wp-content/uploads/2019/12/2012_the_
    looming_taiwan_fighter_gap.pdf
    https://www.defensenews.com/air/2017/12/21/taiwan-fighter-jets-
    get-new-electronic-warfare-capabilities-in-latest-upgrade/

3   https://news.ltn.com.tw/news/politics/breakingnews/2997950

4   https://www.taipeitimes.com/News/taiwan/
    archives/2020/10/30/2003746044
    https://www.the-northrop-f-5-enthusiast-page.info/

    https://focustaiwan.tw/politics/202103230026

5   http://www.taiwanairpower.org/af/c130he.html

6   https://www.hsdl.org/?view&did=683064

7   https://today.line.me/tw/v2/article/%E5%90%8D%E5%AE%
    B6%E8%AB%96%E5%A3%87%E3%80%8B%E6%96%BD%E
    5%AD%9D%E7%91%8B%EF%BC%8F%E9%BB%91%E9%B7
    %B9%E6%8E%A5%E6%89%8B%E8%97%8D%E9%B7%B9+%-
    E3%80%80%E5%9C%8B%E8%BB%8D%E4%BA%9F%E9%9C%80%E7%
    9A%84%E6%88%B0%E5%A0%B4%E6%90%9C%E6%95%91-OZ6OKy?f
    bclid=IwAR3zVBUYl4gXRBwlB09m3xJdEm8edtxBB0AwqsK2gG82-
    nIVr9xBl870Ofuk

Endnotes CHAPTER 5

1   https://www.us-taiwan.org/reports/2012_the_looming_taiwan_
    fighter_gap.pdf
    https://news.ltn.com.tw/news/politics/breakingnews/3488241

2   https://www.ainonline.com/aviation-news/defense/2017-02-16/
    taiwan-confirms-indigenous-jet-trainer-development
    https://www.defensenews.com/global/asia-pacific/2016/08/10/
    taiwan-advanced-jet-trainer-nears-bidding-process/
    https://www.ainonline.com/aviation-news/defense/2019-09-26/
    taiwan-unveils-new-advanced-trainer
    https://euro-sd.com/2020/07/articles/18187/viewpoint-from-taipei-
    first-flight-of-the-brave-eagle/

3   https://project2049.net/2020/06/30/watching-over-the-taiwan-strait-
    the-role-of-unmanned-aerial-vehicles-in-taiwans-defense-strategy/

4   https://www.shephardmedia.com/news/defence-notes/f-35s-taiwan-
    will-us-cross-chinas-red-line/
    https://www.shephardmedia.com/news/defence-notes/taiwan-will-
    push-f-35bs-and-kc-135/
    https://www.defensenews.com/air/2016/01/16/despite-pressures-
    from-china-taiwan-might-procure-harriers/
    http://www.taipeitimes.com/News/taiwan/archives/2017/01/25/2003
    663769competei

5   https://www.taipeitimes.com/News/taiwan/
    archives/2007/06/24/2003366605
    https://www.hsdl.org/?view&did=683064

Further reading

2019 National Defense Report (Taipei: Ministry of National
Defense, ROC)
RUPPRECHT, A., *Modern Chinese Warplanes: Chinese Air Force -
Aircraft and Units* (Houston, TX: Harpia Publishing, 2018)
ISBN 978-09973092-6-3
RUPPRECHT, A., *Modern Chinese Warplanes: Chinese Naval Avia-
tion - Aircraft and Units* (Houston, TX: Harpia Publishing, 2018)
ISBN 978-09973092-5-6

INDEX

THE MOST COMPREHENSIVE AIR ARMS INFORMATION AVAILABLE

AIRFORCES
Intelligence

Constantly
updated and
monitored with
more than
,000 changes
every 3 months

ether your background is in
ary analysis, the defence industry,
ntenance, repair and overhaul
esearch, this is what you need.

esearch and analysis
hreat assessment
ompetitive comparison
eveloping new
arket opportunities

THE ESSENTIAL ONLINE AIR ARMS DATABASE

Comprehensive and accurate data

Profiles for over 380 air arms in 199 countries

Multi-service operations

Secure online access

Downloadable ExcelTM reports

EMAIL: info@AirForcesIntel.com

www.AirForcesIntel.com

ACCURATE TECHNICAL DRAWINGS

IATIONGRAPHIC.COM
+39.338.487.3171
info@aviationgraphic.com
ess: Via Enrico Lai 35, 09128
Cagliari - ITALY

Italian Excellence

AVIATIONGRAPHIC.COM
SINCE 2003

ROYAL AIR FORCE

HARPIA PUBLISHING+

Glide With Us Into The World of Aviation Literature

Modern USMC Air Power | Aircraft and Units of the 'Flying Leathernecks'

Joe Copalman

256 pages, 28×21 cm, softcover

38.95 Euro, ISBN 978-1-9503940-2-9

As America's expeditionary force-in-readiness, the US Marine Corps operates an eclectic mix of fixed-wing, rotary-wing, tiltrotor and unmanned aircraft to support the marine rifleman on the ground. The first two decades of the 21st century have seen an almost complete transformation of the marine air wings, as Cold War-era legacy aircraft yield to digital-age replacements. In Harpia's first book dedicated to a North American air arm, Joe Copalman explains the significance of each aircraft transition in the Marine Corps over the previous 20 years – community by community – on the Marine Air-Ground Task Force and its ability to conduct amphibious and expeditionary warfare.

Flashpoint Russia | Russia's Air Power: Capabilities and Structure

Piotr Butowski

144 pages, 28×21 cm, softcover

24.95 Euro, ISBN 978-0-9973092-7-0

Russian military aviation has undergone several upheavals in the post-Soviet era. There have been two driving forces behind these changes. First, the Russian experience of air power in conflicts has led to an increasing integration of the various branches of the armed forces. Today's VKS was created as a result of the absorption of the Air Defence Troops (VPVO) by the Air Force (VVS) in 1998, and then a merger of the Air Force with the Aerospace Defence Troops (VVKO) in 2015.

The fourth title in Harpia Publishing's series on Russian military aviation details all fixed-wing aircraft, helicopters and other aerial vehicles operated by Russia's military air arms. Like the previous volumes, *Flashpoint Russia* is a comprehensive reference work, presenting organisational structure and the quantitative potential of Russian military aviation.

Modern Chinese Warplanes | Chinese Air Force – Aircraft and Units

Andreas Rupprecht

256 pages, 28×21 cm, softcover

38.95 Euro, ISBN 978-0-9973092-6-3

In 2012 the original *Modern Chinese Warplanes* set the standard as a uniquely compact yet comprehensive directory of modern Chinese air power, combining magnificent illustrations and in-depth analysis. Now almost six years later, much of the fascination that Chinese military aviation holds for the analyst and enthusiast still stems from the thick veil of secrecy that surrounds it. However, in the time that has passed since the first edition, a plethora of new types, systems and weapons has been revealed. What is more, the structure of the People's Liberation Army Air Force (PLAAF) has been completely revised by transforming the former Military Regions into Theater Commands.

THE AVIATION BOOKS OF A DIFFERENT KIND

UNIQUE TOPICS I IN-DEPTH RESEARCH I RARE PICTURES I HIGH PRINTING QUALITY